not another Teen Knitting *book*

Vickie Howell

Photography by Jody Horton

Sterling Publishing Co., Inc.
New York

For Mom

Thanks for sticking with me during my "eventful" teenage years. I love you.

Photography: Jody Horton
Illustrations: Orrin Lundgren
Graphic Artist: Dave Lowe
Book Design: Chris Swirnoff
Project Consultant: Wendy Preston
Editor: Rodman Pilgrim Neumann

Library of Congress Cataloging-in-Publication Data

Howell, Vickie.
  Not another teen knitting book / Vickie Howell ; photography by Jody
Horton.
      p. cm.
  Includes index.
  ISBN 1-4027-2066-1
  1. Knitting--Patterns. 2. Children's clothing. I. Title.

TT820.H8135 2006
746.43'2--dc22

2005024368

2 4 6 8 10 9 7 5 3 1

Published by Sterling Publishing Co., Inc.
387 Park Avenue South, New York, NY 10016
© 2006 by Vickie Howell
Distributed in Canada by Sterling Publishing
c/o Canadian Manda Group, 165 Dufferin Street
Toronto, Ontario, Canada M6K 3H6
Distributed in the United Kingdom by GMC Distribution Services
Castle Place, 166 High Street, Lewes, East Sussex, England BN7 1XU
Distributed in Australia by Capricorn Link (Australia) Pty. Ltd.
P.O. Box 704, Windsor, NSW 2756, Australia

Printed in China
All rights reserved

Sterling ISBN-13: 978-1-4027-2066-6
ISBN-10: 1-4027-2066-1

For information about custom editions, special sales, premium and
corporate purchases, please contact Sterling Special Sales
Department at 800-805-5489 or special sales@sterlingpub.com.

syllabus

Is there any question?

To knit or not to knit . . .

Skaters

Track Meet

I really wanted to write a knitting book for teenagers that wasn't exclusive to one style or set of interests. Even though I graduated (*ahem*) several years ago and I know trends and demands have evolved, daily life most certainly hasn't. Just like a truly well-rounded High School existence, a knitting book representing that experience requires three things: hard work, a sense of humor, and the acknowledgment that without diversity, life would be pretty freakin' mundane. In hindsight, the way that cliques are isolated, judged, and labeled in school is really quite oppressive (it makes me cringe to think about how my "popular" friends often voiced their disapproval of me hanging out with the "drama kids"). In the midst of teenagerhood, however, such elitism seemed not only normal, but essential, to the ebb and flow of socialization.

The projects in the following pages represent different groups, events, and milestones, serving as a microcosm for the stereotypical high school adventure. Set in the context of a yearbook parody, they're as fun to make as they are to use! Hopefully the contributing designers and I have done our part to show that being creative is sexy, and that knitting is every bit as cool as wielding a guitar or riding a snowboard. Self-expression through knitting is sure to set you apart from the cookie-cutter world of manufactured fashion and mediocrity. So whether you're punk, jock, brain, or completely uncategorized, this book will have a little something in it for you. Enjoy!

_Vickie

Roll Call

Jocks

Homecoming Queen

First Car

Drama Club

Best Friends

...ains

Populars

Prom

More Roll Call

Pep Rally

Class Elections

Graduation

Rockers

Goths

Marching Band

Spring Break

Nerd

Preppies

College Bound

Punks

Exchange Student

Granolas

Yearbook Staff

Dance Company

Abbreviations

approx	approximately		**RH**	right-hand
beg	beginning		**rib**	ribbing
BO	bind off		**rnd**	round
CC	contrasting color yarn		**RS**	right side
ch	chain		**sc**	single crochet
CO	cast on		**sl**	slip
cont	continue, continuing		**SKPO**	Slip I st, knit I st, pass slipped st over knit st
dec	decrease, decreasing		**S2KPO**	Slip 2 sts together, knit I st, pass 2 slipped sts over knit st
dpn(s)	double-pointed needle(s)			
inc	increase, increasing			
k	knit			
k2tog	knit two stitches together		**ssk**	slip, slip, knit (slip 2 stitches, then knit them together through the back loop)
LH	left-hand			
MI	make one stitch			
MC	main color yarn			
p	purl		**St st**	stockinette stitch (alternate between knit and purl rows)
pat	pattern			
pm	place marker			
PSSO	Pass slipped stitch over		**st(s)**	stitch(es)
rem	remaining		**tbl**	through the back loop
rep	repeat		**work even**	work in pattern without increasing or decreasing any stitches
rep from *	repeat all the instructions following the asterisk as many times as indicated, in addition to the first time			
			WS	wrong side
			yo	yarn over
			2yo	double yarn over

Grade Level

Project Difficulty Levels

You don't have to be captain of the knitting team or vale-knit-orian of your class to tackle any of the projects in this book. Although some of the patterns do offer more of a challenge than others, they're all designed to be attainable for any beginning to intermediate knitter. So you'll always know exactly what to expect, however, they're each identified by one of the following levels:

FRESHMAN—Very easy
Great first-time or "quickie" projects

J.V.—Moderately easy
Perfect for knitters looking to take their skills up a notch

VARSITY
A bit more challenging, but you can totally do it!

The Basics

CASTING ON
Long-Tail Method

Allow about an inch of yarn per stitch that you'll be casting on; this will be your tail. Letting the tail hang, tie a slipknot around one of your knitting needles. You'll now have two strands of yarn hanging down from your needle (the tail, and the strand connected to the ball). Take the needle in your right hand and with the thumb and pointer finger of your left hand; separate the two strands of yarn. Secure both loose ends under your ring finger and pinky (if you pull the needle down towards your palm, you'll see that loops have formed around both fingers). Take your needle and scoop **under** the outer strand of the thumb loop and then **over** the inner strand of the pointer finger loop. Let the loop fall off of your thumb and pull the tail so that the stitch fits loosely onto the needle. Repeat until you have cast on the desired number of stitches.

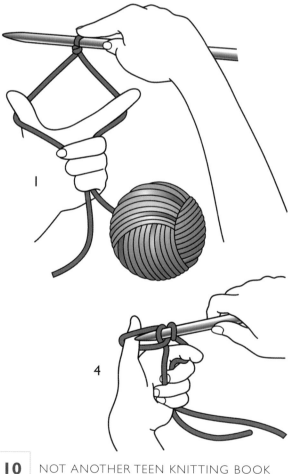

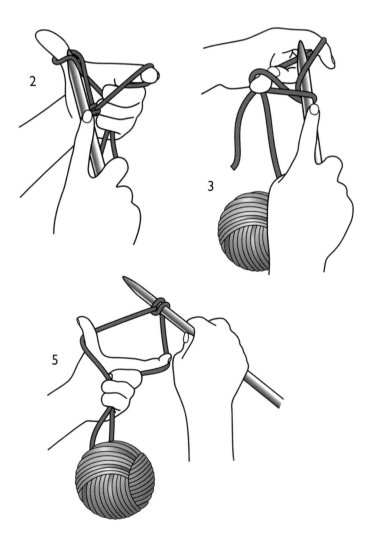

KNIT STITCH
English Method

Hold the needle with the stitches in your left hand. For the knit stitch, working yarn is held in your *right* hand and in the back of the work. Insert your right-hand needle from bottom to top, into the stitch (the tips of your needles will form an "X"). Use your right index finger to wrap the strand of yarn (in a counterclockwise motion) around the right-hand needle. Bring yarn through the stitch with right-hand needle and pull the loop off the left-hand needle. You now have one complete knit stitch on your right-hand needle. Continue until the end of the row or as pattern directs.

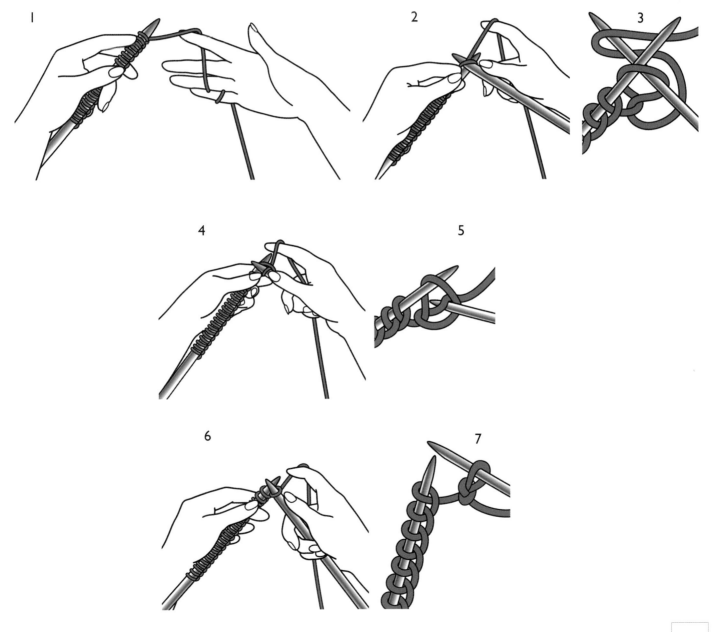

KNIT STITCH
Continental Method

For the knit stitch, the working yarn is held in your *left* hand and in back of the work. Hold the needle with the stitches in your left hand. Insert the right-hand needle from bottom to top, into the stitch (the tips of your needles will form an "X"). Use your left index finger to wrap the strand of yarn (in a coun-terclockwise motion) around the right-hand needle. Bring the yarn through the stitch with the right-hand needle and pull the loop off the left-hand needle. You now have one complete knit stitch on your right-hand needle. Continue until the end of the row or as pattern directs.

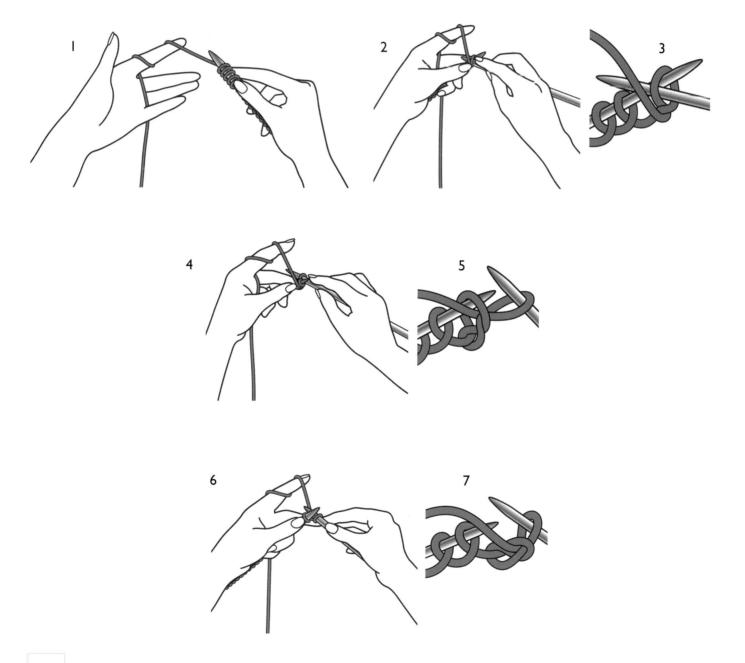

PURL STITCH
English Method

Hold the needle with the stitches in your left hand. For the purl stitch, the working yarn is held in the *right* hand and in front of the work. Insert the right-hand needle from top to bottom, into the stitch. Use your right index finger to wrap the strand of yarn (in a counterclockwise motion) around the right-hand needle. Bring the yarn through the stitch with the right-hand needle and pull the loop off the left-hand needle. Continue until the end of the row or as pattern directs.

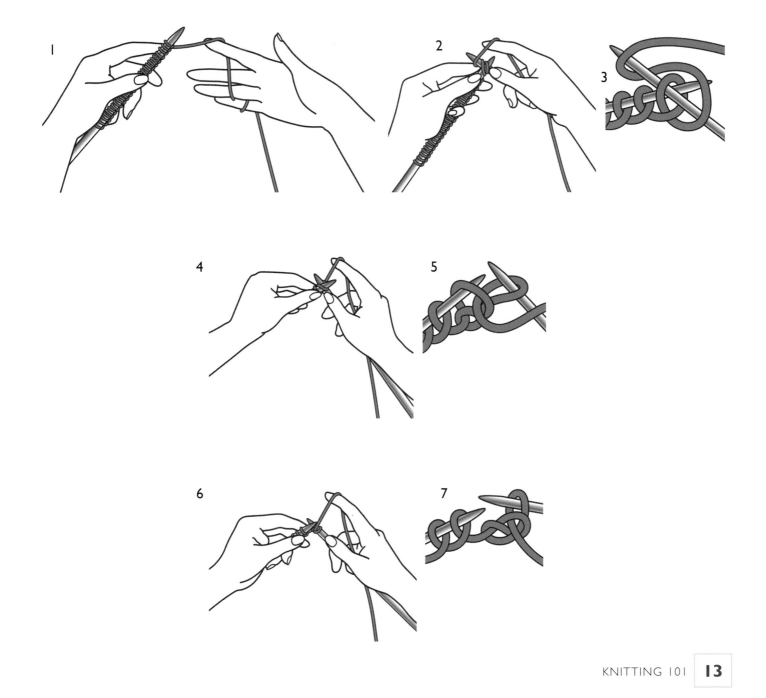

PURL STITCH
Continental Method

For the purl stitch, working yarn is held in the *left* hand and in the front of the work. Hold the needle with the stitches in your left hand. Insert your right-hand needle from top to bottom, into the stitch. Use your left index finger to *wrap* strand of yarn (in a counterclockwise motion) around the right-hand needle. Use the tip of the right-hand needle to scoop the yarn, bringing it through the stitch while pulling the loop off the left-hand needle. Continue until the end of the row or as pattern directs.

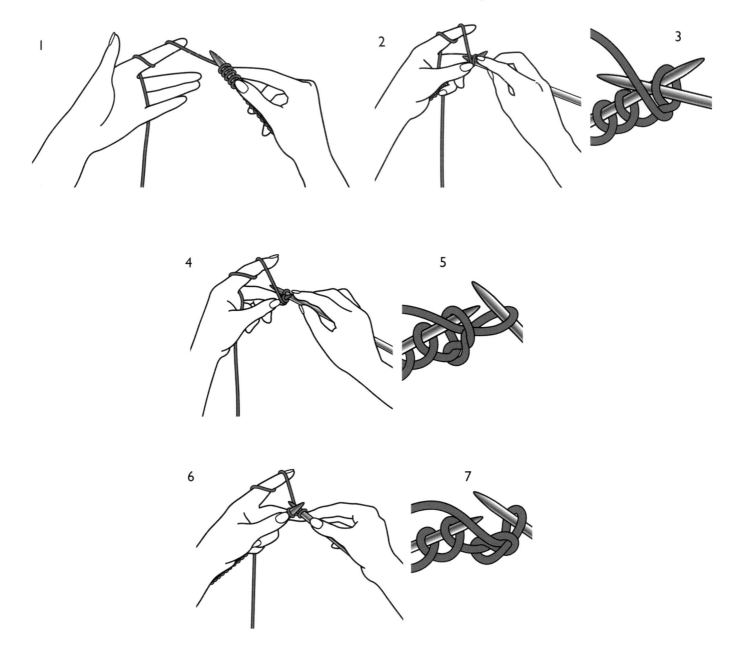

BINDING OFF

Knit two stitches. *With the tip of your left-hand needle, pull the second stitch on the right-hand needle over the first and let it drop off (you'll now have one stitch left on the needle). Knit another stitch and repeat from *. Continue in this manner or as directed by pattern.

1

2

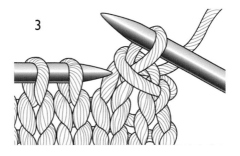
3

WEAVING IN ENDS

Using a tapestry needle, weave loose ends in and out of stitches on the wrong or "nonpublic" side of the work. Whenever possible, weave in ends along seam lines.

INTARSIA

Intarsia is a method of knitting that involves large color blocks. Following a chart, you'll literally knit a simple picture into your garment. Work in the main color, switching to pattern colors as called for by the design. For each section of color, you should use a separate ball or bobbin of yarn to avoid fabric puckering. When changing from one yarn to another, make sure to wrap around the neighboring yarn to avoid holes. Don't worry if your garment doesn't seem to be lying perfectly flat as you're knitting. With intarsia, blocking almost always fixes any misshaping that occurs.

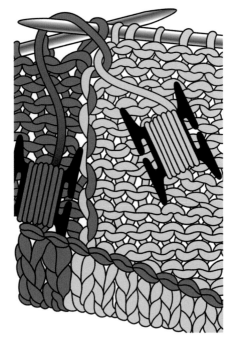

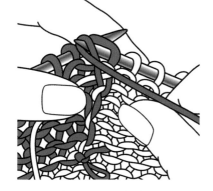

Using bobbins for intarsia knitting

Intarsia knitting with long strands

FAIR ISLE

Fair Isle is a method of knitting that uses two or three different colors in the same row of a project. Instead of joining a new ball of yarn every time the chart calls for another color, you'll instead loosely carry the "inactive" color along the back or "nonpublic" side of the work. The easiest way to do this is to hold one color in each hand (dropping and picking up a third color, if called for), using them both to knit. In other words, you'll be using both the English *and* the continental methods to knit, alternating hands, depending on which yarn is called for. I recommend laying your project out flat every once in a while to check your tension, making sure that no puckering has occurred.

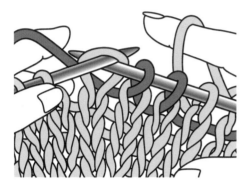

Knitting with right hand, stranding with left

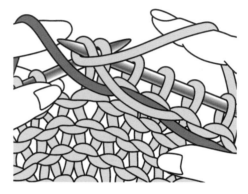

Purling with right hand, stranding with left

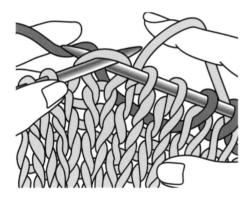

Knitting with left hand, stranding with right

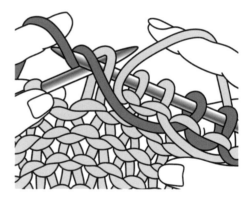

Purling with left hand, stranding with right

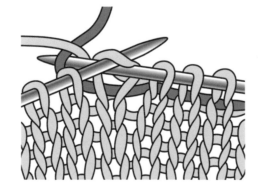

Weaving yarns when changing colors on knit rows

I-CORD

With a double-pointed or circular needle, cast on number of stitches called for. Knit across row. Once that row is complete, slide stitches to the opposite end of the needle and switch hands so that the needle (or end, if you're working with a circular needle) with the knit row is in your left hand. The working yarn will appear to be at the wrong end of the row, but bring it behind the stitches and begin knitting again. The strand of yarn stretched across the back will create a tube. Continue in this manner until you achieve the desired length.

DOUBLE-STRANDING WITH ONE BALL OF YARN

If a project calls for double-stranding but doesn't require the yardage of more than one ball, simply pull a strand from both the beginning and the end of the ball, holding them together as if one strand of yarn. Knit as usual.

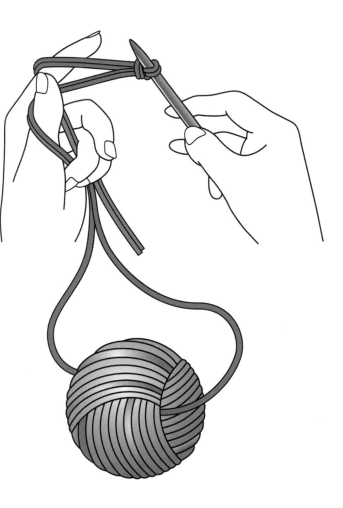

1

2

3

TASSELS: Method A *(Used for "Prom" Wrap)*

Cut three to five strands of yarn (depending on how thick you'd like your tassel) **double** the length of your desired finished embellishment. Holding strands together, fold in half. Insert a crochet hook (any size) through the right side of the edge of your project and lay yarn at the folded point over the hook. Pull the yarn through, from back to front, just enough to create a loop. Set aside the crochet hook and use your hands to fold the loop over the edge of the project, pulling the ends of the yarn through the loop. Pull tight.

1

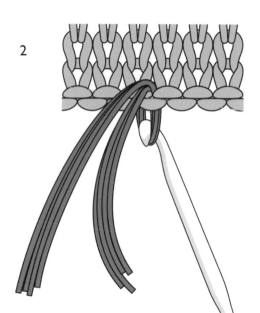

2

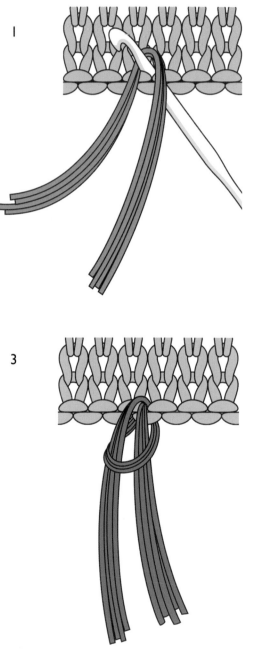

3

4

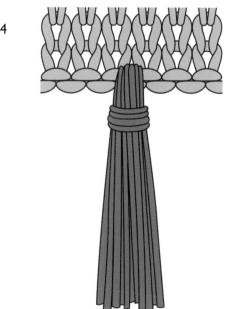

TASSELS: Method B *(Used for Hats)*

Wrap three to five strands of yarn around a CD case (or small piece of cardboard), about 20 to 40 times (depending on weight of yarn). Carefully slide yarn off case and pinch together about an inch down from one end and cinch tightly, using an additional strand of yarn. Cut loops at opposite end, creating tassel strands.

DUPLICATE STITCH

With a tapestry needle and yarn of the same weight as or a slightly finer weight than that of your project, come up through the bottom of the "V" of the knit stitch. Insert the needle under both loops of the stitch above the one you're duplicating, pull the yarn through, and go back down through the point of the "V" where you started.

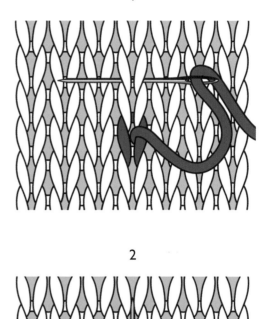

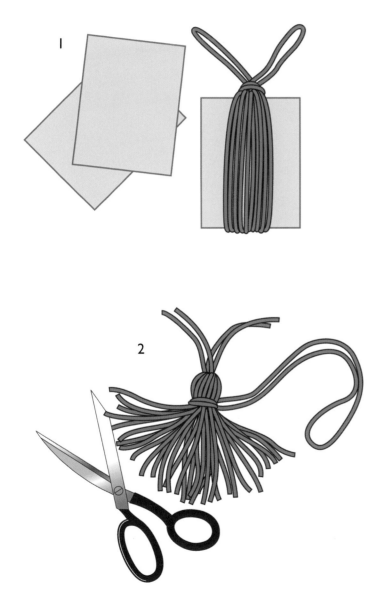

MATTRESS STITCH

Lay the two knitted pieces you want to seam side by side, with the right sides facing you. If you gently pull the edge stitch away from the stitch next to it, you'll notice a row of bars between the stitches. Come up through the back edge of one of your pieces with a tapestry needle and yarn, and insert the needle under one of the bars, pulling the yarn through. Repeat this step on your second piece. Continue picking up bars on alternating pieces, pulling the yarn to close the gap every few stitches. You'll notice your edges slowly beginning to fold inward, creating an almost seamless seam! Continue in this manner until finished. Securely weave in ends.

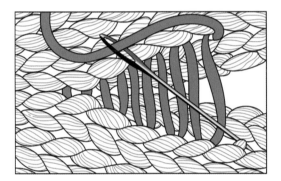

BACKSTITCH

With yarn or embroidery thread and needle, come up through your project at point A. Go back down with needle at point B, up at point C, and then down again through point A. For the next stitch, come up through point D, and back down again through point C. Continue in this manner until your embroidery is the desired length.

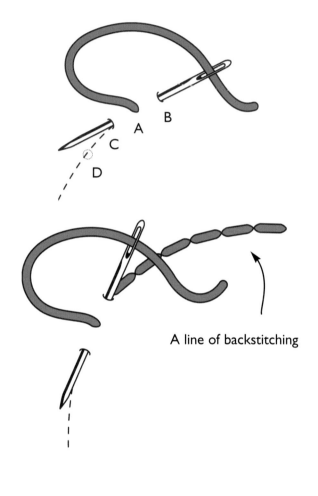

A line of backstitching

FRENCH KNOT

With yarn and tapestry needle, come up through your knitting where you'd like to place your French knot. Wrap yarn around needle twice, pulling the yarn so wraps are tight against the needle. Go back down near the hole that you started from, and pull to create knot.

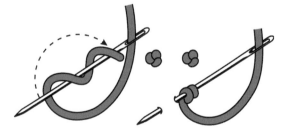

CROCHETED CHAIN

Tie a slipknot onto a crochet hook. This will act as your first stitch. Wrap yarn counterclockwise around the hook and pull through the stitch on the hook. Continue in this manner until your chain is the desired length.

1

2

3

> **Note:** When crocheting a chain, it helps to hold the tail of the yarn securely between your thumb and middle finger while you're working!

SINGLE CROCHET EDGING

Tie a slipknot onto the crochet hook. Insert hook into the front loop of the knitted edge stitch you are embellishing. You now have two loops (stitches) on your hook. Wrap yarn counterclockwise around the hook and draw it through the first loop. Wrap yarn once counterclockwise again, and draw through both loops. Insert hook into the next knit stitch. Wrap yarn and draw through the first loop and then wrap yarn again and draw it through both loops. Continue in this manner until the edging is complete.

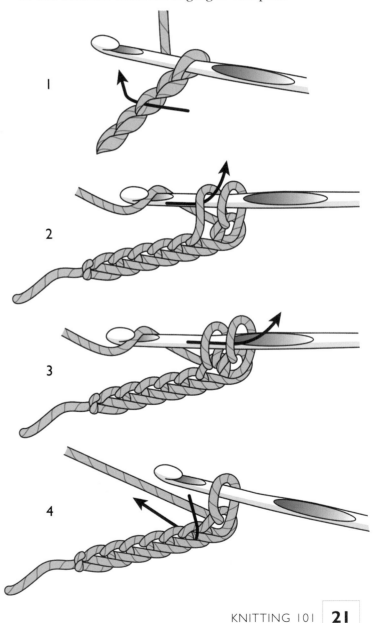

1

2

3

4

POM-POMS

Cut out two cardboard circles as big in diameter as you'd like your pom-pom to be. Working about ½ inch in from the edge, cut out the centers of each circle so the pieces look like donuts. For ease in wrapping yarn, cut both donuts from the outer edge to the center to allow you to slip the yarn into the center as you wrap. Place circles together and begin wrapping yarn around the edge of the circles. Continue in this manner until entire "donut" is covered once or twice over. Place the blade of your scissors **in between** the two layers of cardboard and carefully cut the loops of yarn created by the wrap arounds. Take another piece of yarn and tie the yarn strands between the cardboard pieces together securely. Remove cardboard. Fluff pom-pom and trim if necessary.

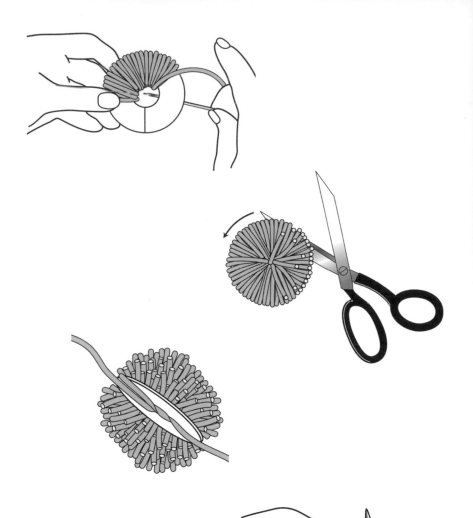

THREE-NEEDLE BIND-OFF

This is a great, secure way to seam together two pieces that still have "live" stitches. Here's how it's done: With the pieces still on their respective needles, place them together with RS facing and needles parallel to each other. Holding the two needles together in your left hand, introduce a third needle with your right hand. BO the two pieces at the same time by inserting the needle through a st on both the front and back needle and knitting them together. Rep 1 more time and then lift the first st on your right-hand needle over the second one, letting it fall off the needle. Continue in this manner until all sts are BO.

Making the Grade

The Projects

Everyone who's anyone will be wearing this scarf!

populars

glam adjustable scarf

VICKIE HOWELL

This scarf uses a conventional stitch with an unconventional "yarn" to create a fun and funky accessory that looks like it just came off the runway. It uses metallic fabric, cut up into strips, adding a little bit of glamour and texture to an otherwise simple pattern. The scarf is designed with multiple keyholes so it can be worn at different lengths, making it look as great with jeans and a T-shirt as it does with a skirt and heels. It's simple, inexpensive, and fabulous. What could be better?

MATERIALS

2 yards metallic novelty fabric

Rotary cutter

Quilter's square

Self-healing mat

US size 17 (12.75 mm) needles

Stitch holder

GAUGE

Approx 8 sts = 4 inches in st st (may vary depending on accuracy of fabric strip)

Making Fabric Yarn

Fold fabric in half and then in half again so you have four layers of fabric. Lining up your fabric on the gridlines of the self-healing quilter's mat, cut fabric into 1-inch strips, using a quilter's square or book as a straight edge to guide you. Don't worry; the strips do not need to be perfect! Tie strips together at ends and wind into ball. You'll notice a lot of fraying at the edges; this will create a great fringed glam look in the finished fabric.

Directions

CO 6 sts. *Knit 12 rows.

K3; place last 3 sts on st holder.

Knit the 3 sts rem on needle for 6 rows. Cut yarn.

Place sts just worked onto holder.

Join yarn and knit sts from first holder for 5 rows. On 6th row, k3 and then cont across row by k3 from rem holder.

Repeat from * until scarf measures 36 inches. Knit 12 rows. BO.

FINISHING

Make sure any ends poking out from your tied strips are firmly knotted. Trim them down to about 2½ inches long so you can see the fringed detail of the fabric.

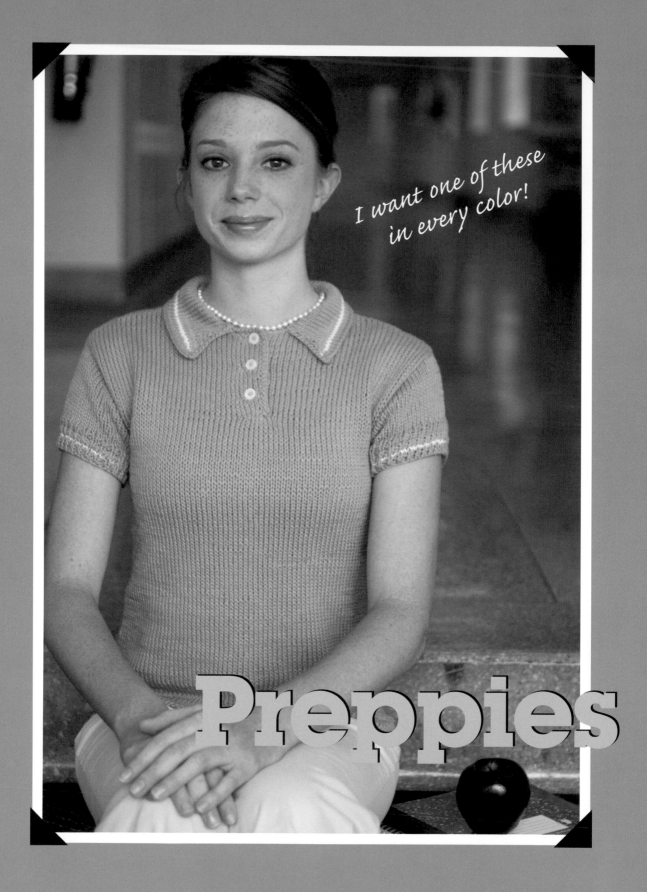

I want one of these in every color!

Preppies

polo shirt

JENNA ADORNO

I wore these shirts when I was a teenager in sunny california in the 1980s. Everyone knew that in high school the coolest way to wear them was layered in bright sherbet colors with the collars standing up. And while I'm not sure I was really preppy in high school (I was both a cheerleader and a field hockey player), my drawer was stuffed with these tops in every color imaginable: some with alligators on them, others embellished with words, a few plain. I have a school photo sporting this look, and I think I even kissed my first boyfriend at a school dance in an ensemble strangely similar to this one. Now that I am old enough to recognize the trend a second time around, I could not resist knitting a testament to my high school days. This unisex polo shirt is a modern takeoff on a classic. The side vents, ribbed cuffs, and button detail give it the perfect preppy vibe, and whether it's 1980 or 2020, the look is timeless.

MATERIALS

Brown Sheep Company Cotton Fleece (80% cotton/20% wool; 215 yds/176m per 100g:

- 3 skeins #CW225, Coral Sunset (MC)
- 1 skein #CW100, Cotton Ball (CC1)
- 1 skein #CW870, Mint Condition (CC2)

US size 6 (4.0 mm) needles (or size needed to obtain gauge)

US size 4 (3.5 mm) needles (or size needed to obtain gauge)

Three small white buttons

Tapestry needle

GAUGE

20 sts = 4 inches

SIZES

XS (S, M, L)

FINISHED MEASUREMENTS

Bust: 30 (32, 34, 36) inches

BACK

With larger needles and MC, CO 75 (80, 85, 90) sts. Beginning with a knit row, work 3 rows in St st. Knit next row (WS) to make turning row. Continue working in St st without further shaping until body measures 15 (15½, 16, 16½) inches from the bottom.

ARMHOLE SHAPING

* (K1, ssk, work to last 3 sts, k2tog, K1. Purl 1 row.) Repeat twice more from *—69 (74, 79, 84) sts. Work without further shaping until back measures 21½ (21½, 22, 22) inches from bottom.

SHOULDER SHAPING

Work 20 (22, 24, 26) sts, attach second ball of yarn, BO center 29 (30, 31, 32) sts, work to end. Working both sides at once, (BO 7(8, 9, 10) sts at each armhole edge twice, BO rem 6 sts once— no sts remain.

FRONT

Work as for back until piece measures 13½ (14, 14½, 15) inches from the bottom. Repeat armhole shaping as for back. When front measures 14 (14½, 15, 15½) inches begin placket shaping. Knit 38 (41, 43, 45) sts, place remaining 31(33, 36, 39) sts on holder, turn, purl back. Continue in St st without further shaping until piece measures ½ inch from start of placket.

Note: Back piece is purposely longer than front.

Buttonhole row (RS): Work to last 5 sts of placket, place buttonhole (yo, k2tog), k3. Work 2 additional buttonholes at 1¼-inch intervals. Work 2 more rows in St st.

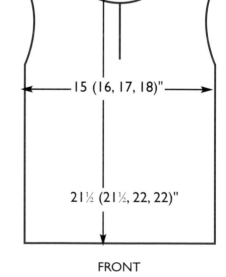

15 (16, 17, 18)"

21½ (21½, 22, 22)"

BACK

15 (16, 17, 18)"

21½ (21½, 22, 22)"

FRONT

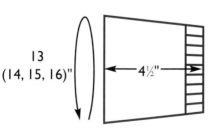

13 (14, 15, 16)"

4½"

SLEEVE

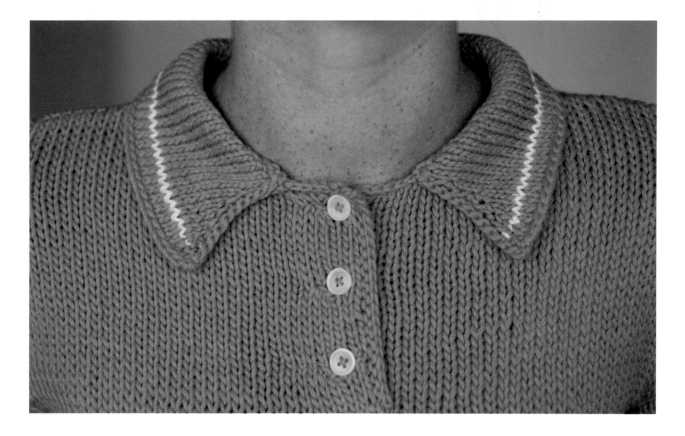

NECK/SHOULDER SHAPING

WS row: At neck edge BO 5 sts once, 4 sts once, 3 sts 3 times. At same distance from back armhole shaping, complete shoulder shaping as for back.

Before reattaching yarn to right side of front, CO 7 sts. Working from right to left, knit rem 31 (33, 36, 39) sts from holder (38, 41, 43, 45 sts total). Continue working even until right- and left-side plackets are same length (approx 3 inches). Complete as for left front, reversing shaping by working neck decs at beg of RS rows and shoulder BO at same distance from armhole shaping.

SLEEVES (MAKE 2)

With smaller needles and MC, CO 52 (56, 60, 64) sts. Work 3 rows in k1,p1 rib. With CC1, work 1 row. With CC2, work 3 rows. With MC and while continuing to maintain pat, work 3 more rows. Change to larger needles. Inc 1 st each edge every 5 rows 3 times—58 (62, 66, 70) sts. Work even until sleeve measures 4½ inches. BO all sts.

COLLAR

Sew shoulders together.

With larger needles, MC, and RS facing, pick up 70 (72, 74, 76) sts around edge of collar. Do not pick up sts along top of placket. Work as follows: RS: *(K1, inc1, work across to last st, inc1, k1. Purl back.) Repeat from *for 12 rows. Change to CC2 and continue as established for 3 rows. Change to CC1, work for 1 row. Change to MC, work 2 more rows. Work 1 turning row. BO.

FINISHING

Pick up sts along edge of placket, purl back, BO. Stitch down bottom of placket to inside edge. Set in sleeves and sew side seams, leaving opening for side vents with longer tail in back. Stitch hems in place. Sew on buttons.

Steam collar to prevent curling.

CRAFT.
ROCK.
LIVE.

riot gRRRLs rule!

Punks

LEVEL: **VARSITY**

fair isle
mini-kilt

VICKIE HOWELL

Although I didn't really hang out with anyone from the "punk" crowd until after I graduated, I always secretly envied their fashion risks and willingness to express themselves through dress. To this day, I have a warm spot in my heart for the 20-hole-Doc-Marten-and-mini-kilt look, so I decided to design my own version of the wee skirt. The juxtaposition of the traditional Fair Isle technique with the irreverence of the punk movement produced a garment that is both girl and gRRRL!

MATERIALS

Berroco Cotton Twist (70% mercerized cotton/30% rayon; 85 yds/78m per 50g ball):

- 1 (1, 2) balls #8390, Pitch Black (MC)
- 2 (2, 3) balls #8311, True Red (CC1)
- 1 ball #8379, Stone (CC2)

US size 6 (4.0mm) circular needle (or size needed to obtain gauge)

US 7 size (4.5mm) circular needle (or size needed to obtain gauge)

Tapestry needle

1 yd black cotton fabric

Black thread

Sewing machine (optional)

2 D-rings

30-inch clasped chain necklace

GAUGE

22 sts = 4 inches in St st

SIZES

S (M, L)

FINISHED MEASUREMENTS

Upper hip: 30 (32, 34) inches

Note: Choose a size approximately 2 inches smaller than your actual measurement. The fabric will stretch to fit.

6½ (6¾, 7)"

Upper Hip
30 (32, 34)"

Cool Tip

When casting on a large amount of stitches, place markers every 20 stitches, to make keeping track of number easier.

SKIRT TOP

With smaller needle and MC, CO 162 (173, 182) sts.

Join rnd, taking care not to twist; pm. Work 5 rnds in k1, p1 rib.

Rnd 6: Switch to larger needle and knit all sts in rnd.

Rnds 7–12: Following chart, begin Fair Isle (see page 33) plaid pat with MC and CC1 (rep all the way around).

Rnd 13 (inc rnd): Cont working in chart pat while inc as follows: work 41 (43, 46) sts, M1, work next 80 (87, 92) sts, M1, work even to end.

Rnds 14–15: Work even, cont to follow chart.

Rnd 16: Work 42 (44, 47) sts in pat, M1, work next 81 (88, 93) sts, M1, work even to end.

Rnds 17–18: Work even, cont in pat.

Rnd 19: Work 43 (45, 48) sts in pat, M1, work next 82 (89, 94) sts, M1, work even to end.

Rnds 20–21: Work even, cont in pat.

Rnd 22: Work 44 (46, 49) sts in pat, M1, work next 83 (90, 95) sts, M1, work even to end.

Rnds 23–28: Work even, cont in pat.

Rnd 29: Work 45 (47, 50) sts in pat, M1, work next 84 (91, 96) sts, M1, work even to end.

Rnds 30–42: Work even, cont in pat to end. Cut CC1.

Rnds 43–44: With MC only, knit.

Rnds 45–46: Purl.

Sizes M (L) only: Purl 2 (4) additional rows.

BO purlwise.

Using CC2, tapestry needle, and duplicate stitch, embroider final plaid lines.

Weave in ends. Block.

Note: CC2 will be used to duplicate stitch the rest of plaid pattern later. Don't worry about carrying long "floats," the loose threads will be tacked down by duplicate stitching.

LOOPS

Measure 3 (3½, 4) inches in from right side of skirt top. With larger needle and MC, pick up 6 sts at base of rib and work even in St st for 1½ inches. BO. Slide D ring onto the strip you've just created, fold strip over, and stitch down to form loop. Repeat for second loop approx 7 (7½, 8) inches from first one.

SKIRT RUFFLE

Cut two 8 x 36-inch fabric strips. Sew short ends together, making one 71½-inch long strip (using ¼-inch seam allowance). Hem bottom by rolling edge over ¼ inch, twice. Press, pin, and stitch.

Baste along raw edge of strip (about ¼ inch down from top). Pull threads on both ends of strip, ruffling fabric. With RS together, fold ruffle in half and seam remaining short ends (using ¼ inch seam allowance) to create skirt bottom. Pin ruffle to the bottom underside of knitted skirt top and sew on either by hand or machine (recommended).

FINISHING

Lace chain necklace through both D-rings, two or three times. Close clasp and arrange chains appropriately.

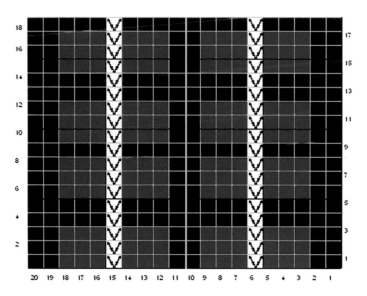

Happy Sweet 16!
Love,
Mom and Dad

First Car

LEVEL: **FRESHMAN**

steering wheel, headrest & seat belt cozies

BETSY McCALL

As with a first love, we all have a special relationship with our first car. How do you express this special connection and really make that vehicle your very own? By cozying up whenever possible! Here are three patterns to celebrate your wheels.

MATERIALS

Seat Belt Cozy

Crystal Palace Yarns Deco-Ribbon (30% nylon/70% acrylic; 80 yds/50g):
- 1 ball #9234, Orange Crush (A)

Crystal Palace Yarns DragonFly (30% nylon/70% acrylic; 44 yds/50g):
- 1 ball #4512, Tomato-Orange (B)

Crystal Palace Yarns Fizz-Stardust (86% nylon/14% soft metallic fiber; 120 yds/50g):
- 1 ball #9517, Nasturtiums (C)

US size 15 (10mm) needles

Headrest Cozy

Crystal Palace Yarns Deco-Ribbon (30% nylon/70% acrylic; 80 yds/50 g):
- 1 ball #9234, Orange Crush (A)

Crystal Palace Yarns DragonFly (30% nylon/70% acrylic; 44 yds/50g):
- 1 ball #4512, Tomato-Orange (B)

Crystal Palace Yarns Fling (95% nylon/5% metallic fiber; 130 yds/50g):
- 1 ball #9492, Nasturtiums (C)

Crystal Palace Yarns Poof (100% nylon; 47 yds/50g):
- 1 ball #9557, Orange Crush (D)

US size 19 (15mm) needles

Steering Wheel Cozy

Crystal Palace Yarns DragonFly (30% nylon/70% acrylic; 44 yds/50g):
- 1 ball #4512, Tomato-Orange (A)

Crystal Palace Yarns Poof (100% nylon; 47yds/50g):
- 1 ball #9557, Orange Crush (B)

Crystal Palace Splash (100% polyester; 85 yds/100g):
- 1 ball #9216, Orangeade (C)

US size 19 (15mm) 26-inch circular needles

Tapestry needle

GAUGE

Approx 9 sts = 4 inches, using any of the yarns triple stranded in garter stitch

FINISHED MEASUREMENTS

Seat Belt Cozy: 13½ x 5½ inches

Headrest Cozy: 16 (at widest point) x 8 inches

Steering Wheel Cozy: 16 inches in diameter

Seat Belt Cozy

CO 30 sts, carrying all three yarns together as one. Work garter stitch (knit every row) for 20 rows. BO.

FINISHING

Fold cozy lengthwise around your seat belt. Use yarn A to sew open edge. If the seat belt cozy slides around too much, secure with a safety pin.

Headrest Cozy

CO 27 sts carrying all four yarns together as one.

Work k2,p1 rib for 5 rows. Break yarn D and cont in rib pat with rem 3 yarns until work measures 8 inches from beg. BO.

FINISHING

Fold in half lengthwise, sewing top and side seams. Piece will resemble a big hat with a Poof (Yarn D) border at bottom edge.

Make 2 tassels and (see page 19) attach both to same side of cozy a few inches in from outer edges. Slide the cozy over the headrest and using a crochet hook or your fingers, pull tassels through (between sts) to other side of cozy. Secure in place.

Steering Wheel Cozy

CO 60 sts, carrying all 3 yarns together as one.

Join. Work 5 rnds in garter stitch (knit every row).

BO.

FINISHING

Looks too big, right? Never fear. Get in your car with the cozy and tapestry needle. Using Splash yarn, sew the cozy around the wheel using a whipstitch. At the points where the arms of the horn attach to the wheel and it isn't possible to close the cozy around the wheel, carry sewing yarn behind the arm and continue on other side. Work your way around the wheel. If there is slack around the circumference, cinch it snug.

Whip Stitch

With yarn and a tapestry needle and from back to front, come up through your piece(s). Go around piece edge(s) and rep in the place where you'd like your next st to be. The closer the reps, the shorter the st lengths.

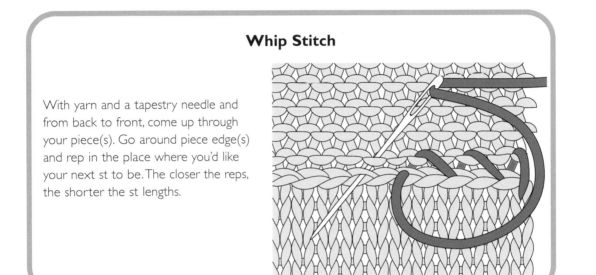

skate or die!

Skaters

LEVEL: **J.V.**

crewneck pullover

JILLIAN MORENO for the Acme Knitting Company

The Autobahn in Germany is the only place in the world where there is no speed limit. That's how skaters view their sport—no limits. I've transformed the highway sign from Autobahn to Skaterbahn. (Bonus points, because it looks like a grind rail.)

MATERIALS

Cascade 220 (100% Peruvian Wool; 220 yds/100g):

- 6 (7, 8) balls #8234, Sage Green (MC)
- 1 ball #2414, Orange (CC)

US size 7 (4.5mm) needles (or size needed to obtain gauge)

US size 6 (4.0mm) 16-inch circular needles (or size needed to obtain gauge)

Tapestry needle

GAUGE

18 sts = 4 inches in St st, using larger needles

SIZES

M (L, XL)

FINISHED MEASUREMENTS

Chest: 45 (49, 53) inches

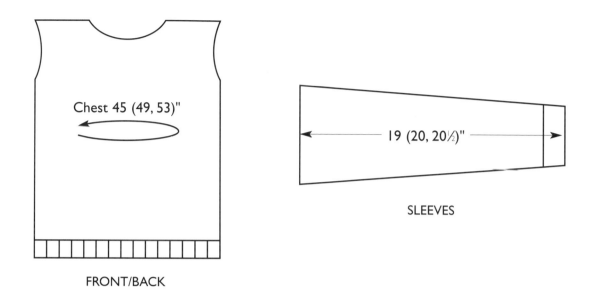

Chest 45 (49, 53)"

FRONT/BACK

19 (20, 20½)"

SLEEVES

BACK

With larger needles and MC, CO 100 (110, 120) sts.

Work in k3,p2 rib pat for 2½ inches.

Switch to St st and work even until pieces measures 26½ (28, 30) inches.

BO all sts.

FRONT

Work as for back, including all shaping and, AT THE SAME TIME, when piece measures 20 (21, 23) inches, attach CC and begin working Skaterbahn chart on center 26 sts.

When piece measures 23½ (24½, 26½) inches, shape neck.

Neck Shaping

On RS row, k40 (46, 50), join second ball of yarn and BO 20 (18, 20), work to end.

Working both sides at once, purl 1 row.

Dec 1 st at each neck edge, every RS row 7 (9, 10) times.

Cont in St st until piece measures same length as back.

BO shoulder sts.

SLEEVES (MAKE 2)

With larger needles, CO 45 (50, 55) sts.

Work in k3,p2 rib for 2½ inches.

Switch to St st, and begin sleeve inc.

Sleeve Shaping

Inc 1 st each side every other row 7 (8, 13) times, then every 4th row 20 (21, 19) times—99 (108, 119) sts.

Cont in St st until piece measures 19 (20, 20½) inches.

BO.

FINISHING

Sew shoulders seams. Place markers 11 (12, 13¼) inches from each shoulder edge. Sew on sleeves between markers. Sew side and sleeve seams. Weave in ends.

With circular needle pick up 90 (95, 100) sts around neck.

Work in k3,p2 rib for 1 inch. BO loosely.

Block sweater if necessary.

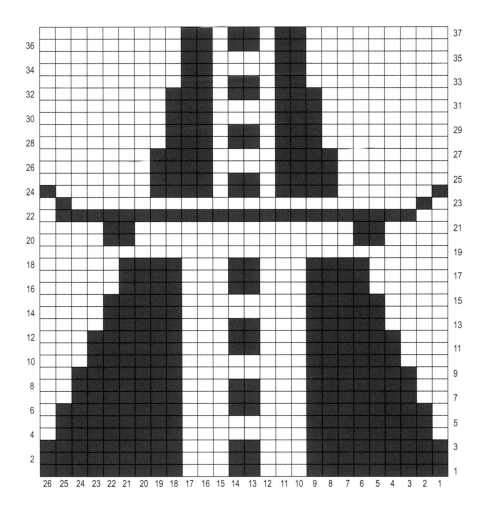

best friends wristbands

VICKIE HOWELL

Gold-plated "Best Friends Forever" charms are so old school. Instead, announce your closest compadre by sporting this modern take on a familiar favorite. Just like the jewelry that inspired them, the motifs on these wristbands form a heart when held side by side. Make the B/F/F set for you and your best bud or, by simply changing the embroidered text to say "True Love," make a T/L/A version for your sweetheart.

MATERIALS

Lion Brand Microspun (100% microfiber acrylic; 168 yds/154m per 2½ oz/70g ball):
- 1 ball #148, Turquoise (MC)
- Small amount of #149, Silver Grey (CC)

US size 6 (4.0 mm) needles (or size needed to obtain gauge)

Orange embroidery floss

Clear beads

Clear sewing thread

Sewing needle

Large-eyed embroidery needle

GAUGE

20 sts = 4 inches in St st

FINISHED MEASUREMENTS

6 x 3½ inches

Make set of 2

With MC, CO 30 sts. Work in k1,p1 rib for 3 rows.

Next row: Switch to St st and work even until piece measures 3 inches from CO edge.

Next RS row: Work 3 rows in k1,p1 rib.

BO in rib pat.

FINISHING

Following chart, count in approx 12 sts from edge (right edge for LH side of heart, left edge for RH side). With CC and large-eyed needle, embroider appropriate side of heart motif into each wristband using duplicate stitch (see page 19).

Use embroidery floss to backstitch (see page 20) "BE FRI" onto the half heart of one wristband, and "ST ENDS" onto the half heart of the other.

With clear thread and sewing needle, sew beads around outside edges of both sides of heart. Sew seam up back of each wristband and weave in ends.

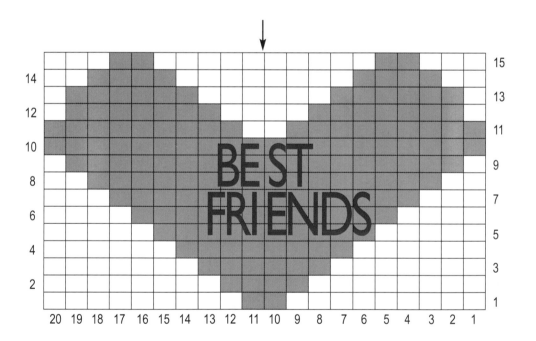

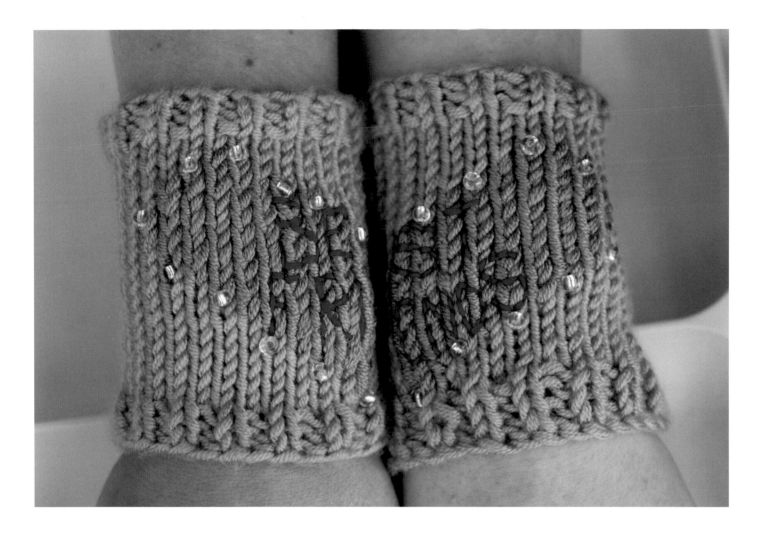

Varsity jackets are required school attire for game days.
—Coach

Jocks

varsity jacket

CHRIS BAHLS

This version of the classic varsity jacket works up quickly with the body and sleeves in a bulky yarn. The striped trim at the collar, cuffs, and bottom is worked in coordinating colors in a worsted weight. Keep it as shown or easily convert this jacket into a letterman's sweater by sewing on your school emblem and sports patches!

MATERIALS

Lion Brand Wool-ease Thick & Quick (80% acrylic/20% wool; 106 yds/97m per 6 oz/170g ball):

- 3 balls #182, Pine (MC)
- 3 balls #402, Wheat (CC1)

Lion Brand Wool-ease Worsted Weight (86% acrylic/10% wool/4% rayon; 197 yds/180m per 3 oz/85g):

- 1 ball #402, Wheat (CC2)
- 1 ball #152, Oxford Grey (CC3)

US size 8 (5.0 mm) needles (or size needed to obtain gauge)

US size 13 (9.0 mm) needles (or size needed to obtain gauge)

Tapestry needle

Five ¾-inch buttons

GAUGE

9 sts x 12 rows = 4 inches in heavier yarn and larger needles

SIZE

Men's M

FINISHED MEASUREMENTS

Chest: 40 inches

Length: 30½ inches

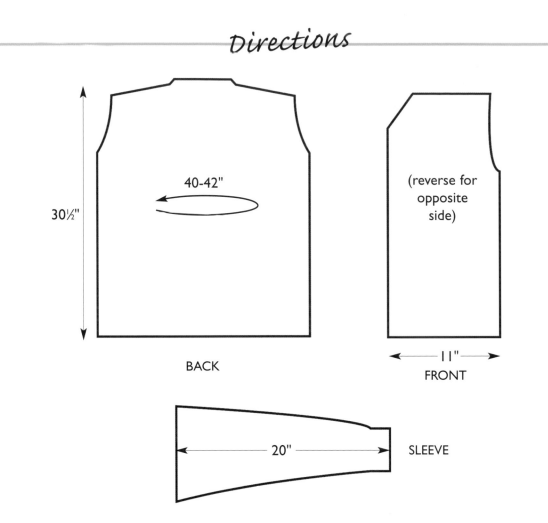

BACK

FRONT
(reverse for opposite side)

11"

SLEEVE

20"

40-42"

30½"

BACK

With MC and larger needles, CO 44 sts. Work in reverse St st (purl RS rows, knit WS rows) for 40 rows or until piece measures 15½ inches.

Armhole Shaping

BO 2 sts at beg of next 2 rows.

Cont until piece measures 26 inches from CO edge (row 70).

On next row, p14, attach second ball of yarn and BO center 16 sts, work to end.

On next row, dec 1 st at each neck edge.

Cont in pat st until piece measures 26½ inches (row 72).

BO rem 13 sts for each shoulder.

FRONT (MAKE 2, REVERSING SHAPING)

With MC and larger needles, CO 22 sts. Work as for back, including all shaping, and, AT THE SAME TIME, when piece measures 3½ inches (row 62) begin neck shaping.

At neck edge, BO 6 sts, work to end. Cont to dec 1 st at neck edge every other row 3 times—13 sts. Work even until same length as back (row 72). BO.

Seam shoulders together with right sides facing. Pm 11½ inches down from shoulder seam on fronts and back.

SLEEVES (MAKE 2)

With larger needle, CC1, and RS facing, pick up 50 sts evenly between markers.

Note: To pick up 2 sts in 1 st of the bulkier fabric, first pull yarn through both loops of BO st, then through front loop only of same st (84 sts).

Work even in St st for 2 rows. Dec 1 st on each side every 5 rows 4 times, then every 6 rows 5 times. Cont in St st until piece measures 17½ inches (row 52).

BO loosely.

COLLAR

With smaller needles, CC2, and RS facing, pick up 24 left front neck sts, 36 back neck sts, 24 right front neck sts. Work 2 rows in k1,p1 rib.

Change to CC3 and work 2 rows in k1,p1 rib. Continue stripe pat for 14 rows total (3 dark stripes), ending with CC2. BO loosely in rib.

CUFFS

With smaller needles, CC2, and RS facing, pick up 2 sts in each BO st of bulkier fabric. Work in k1,p1 rib, alternating, 2 rows of CC2 and CC3 as for collar.

Sew sleeve and side seams.

BOTTOM BAND

With smaller needle, CC2, and RS facing, pick up 2 sts in each BO st of the bulkier fabric. Work in k1,p1 rib, alternating 2 rows of CC2 and CC3 as for collar and cuffs.

BUTTON BAND (RIGHT FRONT)

With larger needle, MC, and RS facing, pick up 59 sts along front edge, including bottom band. Work in St st for 6 rows. End on WS. BO.

BUTTON BAND (LEFT FRONT)

With larger needle, MC, and RS facing, pick up 59 sts along front edge, including bottom band. Work in St st for 3 rows.

Buttonhole row: K2, (k2tog, yo, k11) 5 times, k2.

Continue in St st for 2 more rows, 6 rows total. End on WS. BO.

FINISHING

Sew selvedge edges of collar just inside button band on left and right sides. Sew on buttons opposite buttonholes.

Go Warriors!

Pep Rally

school colors scarf & mittens

STEPHANIE MRSE

This set is perfect for Friday night football games...
whether you are a cheerleader or just a fan. Guys can of course
leave the pom-poms off the scarf. The yarn I've chosen is available in
lots of colors so you are sure to find ones to match your team's. (I made this
set in green and white in honor of my high school—go Hodags!)

MATERIALS

Cascade Yarns 220 (100% Peruvian
wool; 220 yds/100g):

- 2 skeins #TK, Green (MC)
- 2 skeins #8505, White (CC)

US size 6 (4.0mm) double-pointed
needles (or size needed to
obtain gauge)

US size 7 (4.5mm) straight needles
(or size needed to obtain gauge)

Stitch markers

Small stitch holders or safety pins

Cardboard scraps for making
pom-poms

GAUGE

21 sts = 4 inches in St st, using
smaller needles

Special Abbreviations

MIL (make one left):
With left needle tip, lift strand
between needles from front to
back, ktbl.

MIR (make one right):
With right needle tip, lift strand
between needles from back to front,
knit lifted loop through front.

SCARF

With larger needles and MC, CO 40 sts. Work in k2,p2 rib for 30 rows. Change to CC and work 30 more rows. Cont alternating blocks of MC and CC until scarf is approx 6 feet long or desired length, ending with MC. Weave in all ends. Make 6 pompoms (see page 22) about 2 inches in diameter. Sew three to each end of scarf.

MITTENS

With dpns and MC, CO on 40 sts. Arrange evenly over 4 dpns
(10-10-10-10), pm, and join. Work in k2,p2 rib (in the round) for 2¾ inches.

Change to CC and St st. Inc 1 st
at end of next rnd (41 sts).

Note: For the rest of the mitten, you will switch colors every 5 rows.

Shape Thumb Gusset

K20, pm, M1L, k1, M1R, pm, k to end (43 sts).

Knit 1 rnd.

*Knit to marker, slip marker,M1L, knit to next marker, M1R, slip marker, knit to end (45 sts).

Knit 2 rnds even.

Continue from *, inc in
this manner (2 sts every 3 rnds) 5 times—
15 gusset sts between markers.

On next rnd, remove markers and place gusset sts on holder. Make 1 st over gap left by gusset, knit to end of rnd (41 sts).

Work even until St st part of
mitten measures 5¾ inches. On next rnd, dec 1 st (40 sts).

*K8, k2 tog *, repeat around.

Knit 1 rnd even.

Repeat these 2 rnds until 20 sts remain.

Dec 1 st every rnd until 8 sts remain.

Cut yarn, thread tail through rem sts, pull tight, fasten yarn to inside.

THUMB

Place thumb sts on 3 dpns. Pick up 1 st over gap and join (16 sts).

Work in the rnd for 1½ inches from pick up round.

K2tog, k3, k3tog, k3, k2tog, k4 (13 sts).

Knit 1 rnd even.

Continue to dec 3 sts evenly across every other rnd 2 more times until 7 sts remain.

Work 1 more dec row (4 sts).

Cut yarn, thread tail through remaining sts, pull tight, fasten yarn to inside.

Weave in all ends, being sure to close gaps at base of thumb.

I find solace in darkness.

Goths

bat shawl

MELINDA MORROW

A goth-on-the-go may long to look spooky, but scarves and shawls have a way of wandering off the shoulders, ruining the dark perfection of the outfit. The Bat Shawl solves this problem with a knit choker, dramatic points that would do Morticia Addams proud, and convenient places to lace your fingers. Knit on large needles, the shawl will be ready for your next dramatic entrance or night wanderings in no time.

MATERIALS

Bollicine Etoile (70% kid mohair/ 30% Acrylic; 164 yds/50g):

- 4 balls #15, Black (A)

Cascade Yarns Pima Tencel (50% Peruvian pima cotton/50% Tencel; 120 yds/50g):

- 1 ball # 7779, Black (B)

US size 17 (12.75 mm) circular needles, at least 29 inches in length (or size needed to obtain gauge)

US size 6 (4.0 mm) needles (or size needed to obtain gauge)

Tapestry needle

One 3/4-inch button

GAUGE

7 sts = 4 inches in St st, using larger needles and MC doubled

7 sts = 1⅛ inches in garter stitch, using smaller needles and CC

SIZE

One size fits most

FINISHED MEASUREMENTS

65 inches = width at top edge

28 inches = depth at center

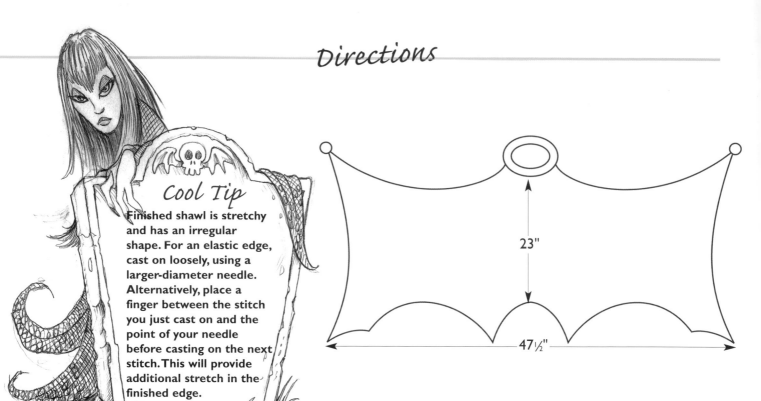

Directions

Cool Tip

Finished shawl is stretchy and has an irregular shape. For an elastic edge, cast on loosely, using a larger-diameter needle. Alternatively, place a finger between the stitch you just cast on and the point of your needle before casting on the next stitch. This will provide additional stretch in the finished edge.

Shawl

With larger needles and MC held doubled, CO 116 very loosely.

Row 1 (WS): Knit across.

Row 2: K1, m1, (k1, m1, k9, ssk, S2KPO, k2tog, k9, m1, k1, yo, k2, yo) 3 times; k1, m1, k9, ssk, S2KPO, k2tog, k9, (m1, k1) 2 times.

Row 3 (and all odd rows until indicated): K1, purl to last st, k1.

Row 4: K1, m1, (k2, m1, k8, ssk, S2KPO, k2tog, k8, m1, k2, yo, k2, yo) 3 times; k2, m1, k8, ssk, S2KPO, k2tog, k8, m1, k2, m1, k1.

Row 6: K1, m1, (k3, m1, k7, ssk, S2KPO, k2tog, k7, m1, k3, yo, k2, yo) 3 times; k3, m1, k7, ssk, S2KPO, k2tog, k7, m1, k3, m1, k1.

Row 8: K1, m1, (k4, m1, k6, ssk, S2KPO, k2tog, k6, m1, k4, yo, k2, yo) 3 times; k42, m1, k6, ssk, S2KPO, k2tog, k6, m1, k4, m1, k1.

Row 10: K1, m1, (k5, m1, k5, ssk, S2KPO, k2tog, k5, m1, k5, yo, k2, yo) 3 times; k5, m1, k5, ssk, S2KPO, k2tog, k85, m1, k5, m1, k1.

Row 12: K1, m1, (k6, m1, k4, ssk, S2KPO, k2tog, k4, m1, k6, yo, k2, yo) 3 times; k6, m1, k4, ssk, S2KPO, k2tog, k4, m1, k6, m1, k1.

23"

47½"

Row 14: K1, m1, (k7, m1, k3, ssk, S2KPO, k2tog, k3, m1, k7, yo, k2, yo) 3 times; k7, m1, k3, ssk, S2KPO, k2tog, k3, m1, k7, m1, k1.

Row 16: K1, m1, (k8, m1, k2, ssk, S2KPO, k2tog, k2, m1, k28, yo, k2, yo) 3 times; k8, m1, k2, ssk, S2KPO, k2tog, k2, m1, k8, m1, k1.

Row 18: K1, m1, (k9, m1, k1, ssk, S2KPO, k2tog, k81, m1, k9, yo, k2, yo) 3 times; k9, m1, k1, ssk, S2KPO, k2tog, k1, m1, k9, m1, k1.

Row 20: K1, m1, (k10, m1, ssk, S2KPO, k2tog, m1, k10, yo, k2, yo) 3 times; k10, m1, ssk, S2KPO, k2tog, m1, k10, m1, k1.

Row 22: K1, m1 (K10, ssk, S2KPO, k2tog, k10, yo, k2, yo) 3 times; k10, ssk, S2KPO, k2tog, k10, m1, k1 (8 sts dec, 108 sts rem).

Row 24: K1, m1, k11, S2KPO, k24, S2KPO, k11, yo, k2, yo, k11, S2KPO, k24, S2KPO, k11, m1, k1 (4 sts dec, 104 sts rem).

Row 26: K1, m1, k11, S2KPO, k22, S2KPO, k11, yo, k2, yo, k11, S2KPO, k22, S2KPO, k11, m1, k1 (100 sts).

Row 28: K1, m1, k11, S2KPO, k20, S2KPO, k11, yo, k2, yo, k11, S2KPO, k20, S2KPO, k11, m1, k1 (96 sts).

Row 30: k1, m1, k11, S2KPO, k18, S2KPO, k11, yo, k2, yo, k11, S2KPO, k18, S2KPO, k11, m1, k1 (92 sts).

Rows 32, 34, 36, 38, 40, 42, 44: K1, m1, k11, S2KPO, k30, yo, k2, yo, k30, S2KPO, k11, m1, k1. Rep this row for a longer shawl.

Row 45: Knit across.

Row 46: K1 (yo, k2tog) 3 times, knit to last 7 sts, (k2tog, yo) 3 times, k1.

Row 47: Knit across.

Row 48: BO loosely.

Note: Depending on how much longer you choose to make your shawl, you may need an additional ball of yarn.

Choker

With smaller needles and CC, CO 7.

Slip 1st st purlwise (with yarn in back), k6. Rep until length equals desired neck measurement.

Buttonhole row: Sl1, k2, yo, k2tog, k2.

Knit 4 more rows, continuing to slip 1st stitch.

BO.

FINISHING

Wash shawl and choker in cool water with mild soap. Blot dry with towels and pin out into desired shape. The shawl's shape should resemble the symbol of a certain famous superhero.

With right sides facing and yarn B, sew the center 7 inches of the choker to the center back of the top of the shawl.

Sew a button on the choker at the end opposite the buttonhole. To wear, thread your fingers or thumbs through any of the eyelets at the ends of the shawl.

Make one for every girl in homecoming court!

Homecoming Queen

award sash

STEFANIE JAPEL

Why wait to be voted most popular or homecoming queen? Instead, claim your own title and knit yourself (or someone special) an award sash. Why not? You deserve it! For the self-confident wearer, drape it across your chest and strut down the school hallway in full "beauty queen" glory. Feelin' a bit shy? Drape the sash around your neck like a scarf and the message will be your little secret.

MATERIALS

Lion Cotton (100% cotton;
    236 yds/212m per 5 oz/140g
    ball)
    • 1 ball #112, Poppy Red (MC)
    • 1 ball #153, Black (CC)

US size 7 (4.5mm) circular needle,
    36 inches in length (or size
    needed to obtain gauge)
Tapestry needle

GAUGE

16 sts = 4 inches in MC and
    garter stitch

FINISHED MEASUREMENTS

Length: 25 (30, 35, 40, 45) inches
Width: 3½ inches

Seed Stitch

Row 1 (RS): K1, *p1,k1; repeat from * to end.

Row 2 (WS): Knit the purl sts and purl the knit sts.

Repeat row 2 for seed st.

Note: When changing color, twist yarns on WS to prevent holes in work.

Wind a small ball or bobbin of CC yarn and set aside for later use in trim.

Using remaining ball of CC yarn, CO 201 (241, 281, 321, 361) sts, placing removable st marker around center stitch.

Rows 1–2: Work even in seed st.

Row 3: Work in seed st to st before marker. Maintaining pattern, p3tog, work seed st to end.

Rows 4–5: Work even in seed stitch.

Row 6: Still using CC yarn, work 3 seed sts. Without cutting CC, join MC and knit to one st before center st, k3tbl. Knit to last 3 sts. Attach smaller CC ball and work rem 3 seed sts.

Row 7: Using the CC yarn, work 3 seed sts, change to MC yarn, and purl to last 3 sts. Change to

CC yarn and work 3 seed sts. Three seed st border (S3) continues in CC through row 22.

For Fair Isle knitting (see page 16), begin working letters on this row according to the directions below. For duplicate stitch (letters to be added later), continue pattern as established in the first 7 rows as follows:

Row 8 (RS): S3, change to MC yarn and knit to last 3 sts, S3.

Row 9: S3, change to MC yarn and purl to one st before the center st, p3tog. Purl to last 3 sts, S3.

Row 10: S3, change to MC yarn and knit to last 3 sts, S3.

Row 11: S3, change to MC yarn and purl to last 3 sts, S3.

Row 12: S3, change to MC yarn and k to one st before center st, k3tbl. Knit to last 3 sts, S3. Rows 13–24: Repeat rows 7–12 twice.

Repeat.

Row 25 (WS): Using CC across entire row, S3, purl to last 3 sts, S3.

Cut yarn from balls not currently in use.

Row 26–30: Work even in seed stitch.

Row 31: BO in seed stitch. (*K1 st, p1 st, pass the knit stitch over the purled stitch and pass off needle. K1 st. Pass the purled stitch over the knit stitch and pass off needle. Repeat from *.)

Cool Tip

For each additional five inches in length, cast on 40 extra stitches. You will need a longer needle for the longer lengths.

FINISHING

Plan what you want your sash to say. Using the chart, determine how many spaces (stitches) are required for each letter. Most of the letters are nine stitches wide. Some of them (M, Q, W, for example) are larger, and some (I) are narrower. So be sure to count when figuring the total width of your word.

Be careful to use only as many letters as will fit on your sash.

You don't want to get to the end and run out of room!

You can use the following guideline: 25 (30, 35, 40)-inch sashes have 124 (134, 144, 154) stitches available for lettering.

Space the letters so there are two stitches between letters and six stitches between words.

Space words evenly left—to—right.

For Example

"President" requires 81 stitches for the letters, and 16 stitches for spaces between the letters, for a total of 97 stitches. If I were making the smallest sash, I would skip 13 stitches, then start the lettering, leaving 14 at the other end.

If too much of the background color shows through after completing the duplicate stitch, you can go over the lettering with a permanent marker.

Weave in ends and block if necessary.

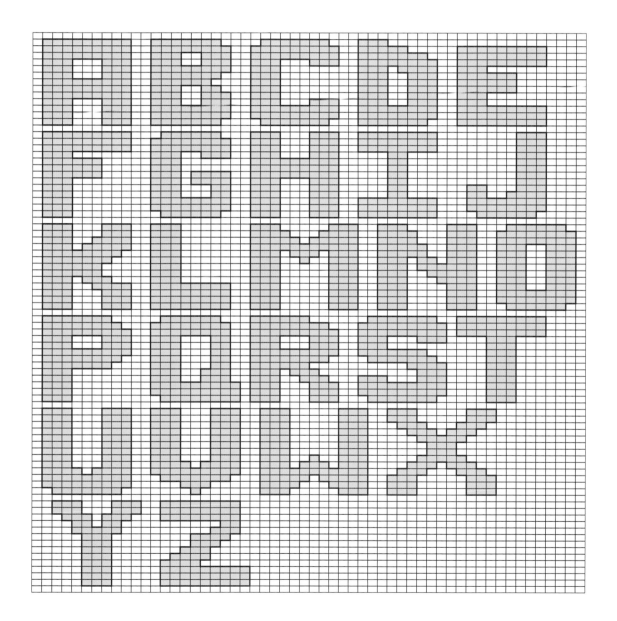

LEVEL: **J.V.**

sweater vest

VICKIE HOWELL

One of my favorite comedians suggests that leather jackets are cool but leather vests are not. The difference between cool and lame, he says? Sleeves. The same could be argued for sweaters. The thing is, though, I secretly love sweater vests despite their lack of hipster sleeve-ness. Oh—and this is no secret—I also have a weakness for nerds. Although this project may seem a little stereotypical, it's really just my own ode to geeky high school outcasts. If only I had known then what I know now...

MATERIALS

Lion Brand Wool-Ease Chunky
 (80% acrylic/20% wool;
 153 yds/140g)
  • 3 (4, 4) balls #152, Charcoal
 (MC)
  • 1 ball #130, Grass (CC1)
  • Scraps of #115, Bay Harbor
 (CC2)
US size 8 (5.0mm) needles (or
 size needed to obtain gauge)
 and 22-inch circular needle
Tapestry needle

GAUGE

12 sts and 16 rows = 4 inches
 in St st

SIZES

S (M, L)

FINISHED MEASUREMENTS

Chest: 36 (38, 40) inches

FRONT

With MC, CO 56 (58, 60) sts. Work in k2,p2 rib for 2½ inches. Work in St st until piece measures 16 (16¾, 17½) inches, ending with WS row.

Armhole Shaping

BO 4 sts at beg of next 2 rows. Work 2 rows even in St st.

RS: K1, ssk, knit to last 3 sts, k2tog, k1.

WS: Purl.

Work 2 rows even in St st.

RS: K1, ssk, knit to last 3 sts, k2tog, k1—44 (46, 48) sts.

WS: Purl**

Work 2 rows in St st.

Left Neck Shaping

RS: K22 (23, 24), place remaining sts on holder.

WS: P 22 (23, 24).

RS: K19 (20, 21), k2tog, k1.

WS: Purl.

Rep last 2 rows 12 times—10 (11, 12) sts rem. BO.

Rep for right neck, reversing shaping.

BACK

Work as for Front until **.

Work in St st until piece measures 25½ inches (26¾ inches, 27½ inches), ending with WS row.

Note: Shoulder sts from both sides remain on needle.

RS: K10 (11, 12), BO center 24 sts, knit to end.

WS: BO 10 (11, 12) sts. Break yarn. Rejoin yarn and BO rem sts.

FINISHING

Argyle Detailing

With CC1 and CC2, duplicate stitch following chart. I put one argyle emblem on the left side of the chest, but really, more than one placed anywhere on the vest could work!

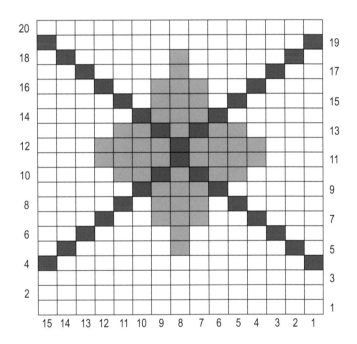

Sew shoulders and side seams. Weave in ends.

Armhole Edging

Pick up 72 (78, 82) sts around armhole. Work 3 rows in k1,p1 rib. BO in rib.

Block if necessary.

A vote for me is a vote for better cafeteria food!

Class Elections

felted bag

VICKIE HOWELL

When you're campaigning for student government, name recognition is the key to a successful race. Come election time, you want voters to know exactly who you are and what office you're running for. With this felted promotional bag, you can make yourself a walking billboard *and* have a place to hold oodles of "Vote for Me" buttons!

MATERIALS

Crystal Palace Yarns Iceland 5 (100% wool; 109 yds/100g):
  • 4 balls #0008, Red Cerise
US size 15 (10mm) circular needles, 29 inches in length (or size needed to obtain gauge)
Handful of black roving
Felting needle
Foam square
Cardboard letter stencils
52-inch piece of mesh strapping
Thread
Sewing machine with heavy-duty needle (optional)
Washing machine
Gentle detergent

GAUGE

14 sts = 4 inches in St st (unfelted)

FINISHED MEASUREMENTS

Before felting: 16 × 22 inches
After felting: Approx 11½ × 12 inches

FINISHING

Seam bottom closed. Machine felt (see page 69), rep until stitch definition has almost disappeared.

Using letter stencils (available at craft stores), spell out desired slogan. Once you're satisfied with letter placement, needle felt (see page 69) text onto bag.

Pin the mesh strapping to inner sides of bag. Attach by top stitching.

BODY

CO 84 sts. Join, taking care not to twist. Knit all rnds until piece measures 22 inches.

Next rnd: K21, BO 42 sts, slip rem sts to LH needle.

FLAP

Work the remaining 42 sts flat (not in the rnd) in St st until flap measures 12 inches. BO.

Cool Tip

The felted fabric is very thick. Make sure you use a heavy-duty needle if machine-stitching and a thimble if sewing by hand.

Needle Felting

Place a two-inch foam block inside your project, directly under the spot you want to embellish. Lay out your stencil(s) and once you're satisfied with their placement, use a size 38 felting needle to lightly stab a small amount of roving into place. Slowly begin adding more roving, making sure the fiber is situated exactly where you'd like it. Stab roving repeatedly, permanently attaching it to the project. Repeat the process until the design is complete.

Machine Felting

Place the knitted project in a zippered pillowcase or fine mesh bag. Throw the bag into the washing machine along with an old pair of jeans or a towel (this will help with agitation) and wash with hot water, omitting the "spin" portion of the washing cycle. Repeat as many times as necessary to achieve the desired result. Take care to check on your project every five minutes or so. When finished, squeeze out excess water, shape per pattern instructions, and let dry on a towel. *Keep in mind that felting will work only with natural, animal fibers that HAVE NOT been "superwash" treated.*

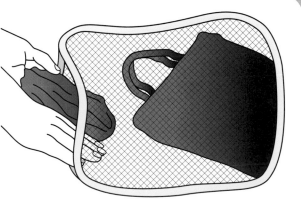

Do you have a prepared monologue?

Drama Club

theater mask hats

LORI STEINBERG

When I was a theatrical teenager, I loved retro things like stocking caps. I also had a collection of jewelry representing the comedy/tragedy masks. Thinking about these things, I drew a mask onto a stocking cap and saw that the eyeholes could actually form the smile or frown of a pair of theater masks. The face of the mask wearer can itself be tragic or comic as the mood suits

MATERIALS

Brown mask version:

Cascade 220 Tweed (90% Peruvian wool/10% Donegal tweed; 220 yds/100g):

- 1 skein #7612, Mocha Tweed (MC)
- 1 skein #7607, Turquoise Tweed (CC1)

Crystal Palace Yarns Merino Frappe (80% Merino wool/20% Nylon; 140 yds/50g):

- 1 ball #031B, Cranberry (CC2)
- 1 ball #146, Cherry Pie (CC3)

Crystal Palace Yarns Deco-Stardust (55% Lurex/ 45% nylon; 118 yds/50g):

- 1 skein #4000, Silver (CC4)

Yellow mask version:

Cascade Yarns 220 Tweed (90% Peruvian wool/10% Donegal tweed; 220 yds/100g):

- 1 skein #7600, Yellow Tweed (MC)
- 1 skein #7601, Green Tweed (CC1)

Crystal Palace Yarns Merino Frappe (80% Merino wool, 20% nylon; 140 yds/50g):

- 1 ball #124, Blueberry (CC2)
- 1 ball #102, Cornflower (CC3)

Crystal Palace Yarns Deco-Stardust (55% Lurex, 45% nylon; 118 yds/50g):

- 1 skein #4000, Silver (CC4)

US size 6 (4.0mm) needles for flat and circular knitting (or size needed to obtain gauge)

US size 7 (4.5mm) needles for circular knitting (or size needed to obtain gauge)

Size J crochet hook

Tapestry needle

Stitch markers

GAUGE

18 sts = 4 inches in St st with larger needles and MC

SIZES

XS/S (M/L)

FINISHED MEASUREMENTS

Circumference: 18–20 (21–23) inches

Length: 21 (24) inches from brim to tail

BO 3 sts, work next 6 sts (7 sts on needle after left eye).

Row 17: Sl1 purlwise, ssk, work 4, break yarn leaving 16-inch tail. Wind off 48 inches of yarn, join yarn to center side of 3. BO sts. Work 8 (11) sts in pattern, CO 1 st. Wind off 60 inches of yarn, join to outside of right eye by making slipknot and sliding it onto RH needle. Work 2 sts in pat, k2tog, k1tbl (5 sts on needle after right eye).

Seed Stitch

Mask is worked flat in seed st, with an edge st made by slipping first st of each row purlwise and knitting last st of each row through the back loop.

Row I(RS): K1, *p1,k1; repeat from * to end .

Row 2 (WS): K the purl sts and p the knit sts.

Repeat row 2 for seed st.

Mask

Changes for large mask are given in parentheses.

With larger needles and MC, CO 44 (47) sts.

Row 1: Sl 1 purlwise, k1, p1 (to last 2 sts, k1,) k1tbl.

Row 2: Sl 1 purlwise, (k1, p1 to last st, k1tbl,) p1,k1, to last 2 sts, k1, k1tbl.

Row 3: Sl 1 purlwise, ssk, k1, p1 to last 3 (4) sts (k1) k2tog, k1tbl.

Rows 4–15: Cont as established, dec both ends on odd-numbered rows (a marker or safety pin will help keep track of odd-numbered rows)—end row 15 with 30 (33) sts on needle.

Row 16: In established pat work 5 sts. Start shaping right eye: BO next 7 sts. Work next 7 (10) sts (8 [11] sts on needle between eyes). Start shaping left eye:

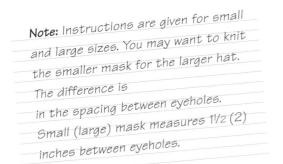

Note: Instructions are given for small and large sizes. You may want to knit the smaller mask for the larger hat. The difference is in the spacing between eyeholes. Small (large) mask measures 1½ (2) inches between eyeholes.

Row 18: Sl1 purlwise, work 4 sts, CO 1 st, drop yarn (6 sts). Pick up center strand, CO 1 st to RH needle, k (p) 1, work 6 (9) sts, k2tog, drop strand (9 [12] sts in center) pick up outside strand, BO 1 st, work 4 (5 sts).

Row 19: Sl1 purlwise, ssk, k2tog, drop strand. With center strand BO 1 st, work 2 (3), BO 1 for nose opening, work 3 (5) in pat, drop yarn. Pick up outside strand, work 3, k2tog, k1tbl.

Row 20: Sl1 purlwise, ssk, p1, k1, CO 3 sts. With same strand, work next 2 (4) sts, k2tog, rejoin yarn on other side of nose opening and BO 1 st, work 1 (2), CO 7 sts. With same strand, k2tog, k1tbl.

Row 21: Sl 1 purlwise, ssk, (k1, p1) 3 times, k1, k2tog, drop strand. Pick up other strand, ssk, (k1,p1) twice (3 times) k1, k2tog, k1tbl.

Row 22: Sl 1 purlwise, (ssk), work 5, k2tog, drop yarn. With other strand, ssk, work 5, k2tog, (k 1tbl).

Row 23: Sl 1 purlwise, work 4 (5), k2tog, drop yarn. With other strand, ssk, work 4 (5), k1tbl.

Row 24: BO 5 (7) sts on both sides.

Weave in ends carefully, remembering that both sides of mask will be "public." Keep marker for odd-numbered rows in place as reference point until finishing is complete.

FINISHING

With crochet hook and CC1, slip st around eyeholes using side without marker as "right" side. Weave in ends, remembering that both sides of mask are "public."

Thread tapestry needle with CC4. Starting at one corner, and leaving a 6-inch tail on each end, embroider a running st around edges of mask, omitting CO edge. Leave ends on side of mask with marker.

Three Suggestions Before Starting Cap

Suggestion 1: The pattern isn't complicated, but familiarize yourself with the color patterns before starting, because the shaping starts one inch into the color pattern.

Suggestion 2: Mark the decrease round by putting a safety pin or plastic marker right into the loop of the stitch, so you can keep track of when the next decrease round should come.

Suggestion 3: Because the Merino Frappe yarn (CC2 and CC3) hides decreases nicely, I tried to have the decrease rounds fall into those stripes. Feel free to fudge a bit to make this happen once the first couple of decreases are completed in CC1. The Stocking Cap is knitted in two basic color patterns—I call them the "color bands pattern" and the "stripes pattern." The color bands are done in two different color ways and alternate to make up the main pattern of the hat.

Stocking Cap

Changes for larger size given in parentheses.

Color Band 1 (CB1)

Rnds 1–5: CC1.

Rnd 6: CC4.

Rnds 7–8: CC2.

Rnd 9: CC4.

Rnds 10–14: CC1.

Rnd 15: CC4.

Cool Tip
Break all strands after each color band to avoid tangling yarn.

Using smaller dpns or circular needles and CC1, CO 90 (100) sts. Join rnd, pm. In k1,p1 rib, work 14 rnds (approx 2 inches).

Switch to larger needles and knit 1 rnd of St st in CC1.

BEGIN KNITTING rnds 6–15 of CB1 (you will begin shaping within this first band—see below). Knit 1 complete CB2 (rnds 1–15), and a second complete CB1 (rnds 1–15). Switch to SP for 1 rep (large hat—2 rep starting second repeat with rnd 3). Knit 1 rnd in CC4 and return to alternating color bands beginning with CB1. Complete 5 color bands, ending with CB1 after first section of SP.

AT THE SAME TIME, begin SHAPING: 1 inch from top of rib, dec 5 sts evenly across rnd. After 1 more inch, repeat dec rnd—80 (90) sts. Knit 14 (21) rnds even. On next rnd, dec 6 sts evenly—74 (84) sts. Continue in color pattern as established for 13 rds. On 14th rnd and following 17th (19th) rnd, dec 6 sts evenly—62 (72) sts. Continue in CB pattern and dec 6 sts evenly every 15th rnd for 5 complete alternating CBs after the first SP—38 (48) sts.

Change back to SP.

Color Band 2 (CB2)

Rnds 1–5: MC.

Rnd 6: CC4.

Rnds 7–8: CC3.

Rnd 9: CC4.

Rnds 10–14: MC.

Rnd 15: CC4.

Stripes Pattern (SP)

Rnds 1–2: MC

Rnds 3–4: CC2

Rnds 5–6: CC3

Rnds 7–8: CC2

Rnds 9–10: MC

FINISHING

Using seam of hat as center back, sew mask to center front of hat. With marker side of mask facing right side of hat, sew CO edge of mask, stitch for stitch, to CO edge of hat ribbing.

Embroidery Band

The band of silver dashes on 1st stripe of MC in 1st rep of CB2, should suggest eyes when mask is in its flipped up position. To place dashes, lay hat on flat surface with mask flipped up. Find st in middle row of MC stripe corresponding to center of mask.

Starting 1 (2) sts over to the right, using CC4 and a tapestry needle, make dash by sewing one horizontal st that covers 3 knitted sts. Skip 5 sts and make dash. Skip 7 sts, make dash, skip 7, make dash, skip 5, make dash, skip 3 (5), make dash, skip 5, make dash, skip 7 (8), make dash, skip 7 (8), make dash, skip 5, make dash.

Star

In duplicate stitch, follow chart, using tapestry needle and CC4. Start about 5 sts from back center on 2nd row of SP at tip of hat (last row of 1st repeat on larger hat).

Make tassel (see page 19) and sew to tip of hat with MC.

Weave in all ends. Press under damp cloth.

Large Hat Only: Work 2 rep of SP, starting 2nd rep as before with rnd 3. IN 1st REP, dec 5 sts in rnd 4, 3 sts in rnd 6, and 2 sts in rnd 10. Complete 2nd rep, rnds 3–10, with no further shaping—38 sts.

Continuing in MC on final 38 sts, *k2, k2tog, rep from *, end k1, knit last st of rnd tog with 1st st of next rnd. Knit 1 rnd even.

Next rnd: K2tog 14 times. Cut yarn, leaving 15-inch tail. Thread tail through tapestry needle and draw through rem sts twice.

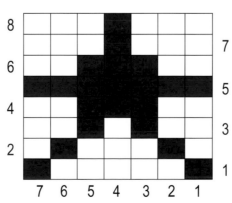

Heads up, shoulders back, toes pointed . . .

Dance Company

wrap sweater & leg warmers

JENIFER PAULOUSKY

Arts have always run strong in my family. I was a drama brat, dancing and singing my way through high school, and now my 15-year-old cousin, Samantha, is an avid dancer. This sweater was originally inspired by the ballet wraps she wears, but I wanted to create something any artist would love. By making the wrap into a pullover, I've made the style more accessible. These yarns are super-soft and come in a million colors, making the possibilities endless—especially if, like me, you're more punk than ballet.

MATERIALS

Leg Warmers

Cascade Yarns 220 Superwash (100% washable wool; 220 yds/100g):

- 1 skein #817, Off-White (MC)

Filatura Di Crosa Baby Extra Kid (80% kid mohair/20% nylon; 269 yds/25g):

- 1 ball #435, Teal (CC)

US size 7 (4.5mm) circular or double-pointed needles (or size needed to obtain gauge)

Tapestry needle

Row counter (recommended)

Sweater

Cascade Yarns 220 Superwash (100% washable wool; 220 yds/100g):

- 3 (4, 5) skeins #817, Off-White (MC)

Filatura Di Crosa Baby Extra Kid (80% kid mohair/20% nylon; 269 yds/25g):

- 2 (3, 4) balls #435, Teal (CC)

US size 3 (3.25mm) circular or double-pointed needles (or size needed to obtain gauge)

US size 8 (5.0mm) circular or double-pointed needles (or size needed to obtain gauge)

Stitch markers

Stitch holders or scrap yarn

GAUGE

28 sts = 4 inches in St st, using smallest needles and CC

20 sts = 4 inches in St st, using largest needles and MC

SIZES

S (M, L)

FINISHED MEASUREMENTS

Leg Warmers: One size fits most

Sweater: Chest—30, fits 30–34 (33, fits 33–37; 36, fits 36–40) inches

Waist—28 (31, 33) inches

Special Abbreviations

KMC—knit across next main color section

PMC—purl across next main color section

(k,p,k)CC—knit across, turn and purl back across, turn again and knit across contrast color section

KCC—knit across contrast color section

PCC—purl across contrast color section

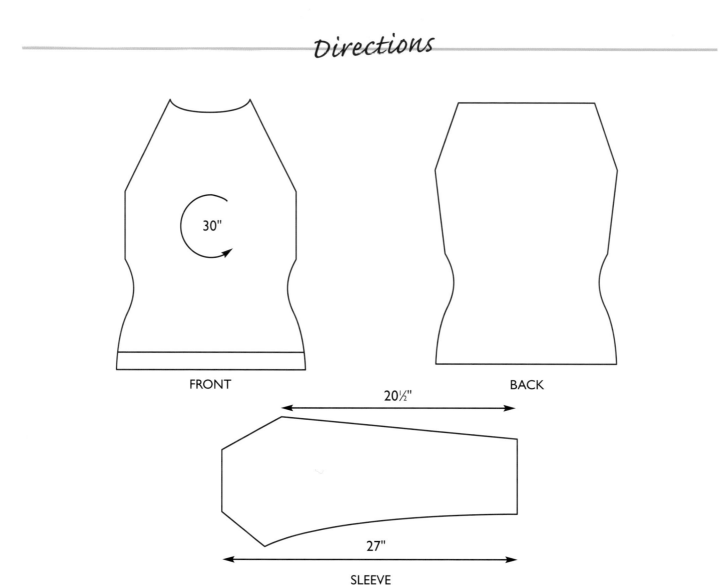

FRONT

BACK

20½"

27"

SLEEVE

Leg Warmers

With US size 7 needles and MC, CO 66 sts and join rnd. Work 10 rnds in k2,p1 rib.

Change to St st: Knit 6 rnds MC, 1 rnd CC, 3 rnds MC, 2 rnds CC, 2 rnds MC, 3 rnds CC, 1 rnd MC.

Change to CC and cont in St st until piece measures 11 inches from CO edge.

Break CC and cont in St st with MC until piece measures 15 inches from CO edge.

Next rnd: Inc 6 sts evenly over rnd (72 sts).

*Pat rnd 1: (K3, p3) to end of rnd.

Pat rnd 2: (P3, k3) to end of rnd.

Rep from * 3 times (6 rows total). BO loosely in pattern.

Sweater

SLEEVE (MAKE 2)

With CC and smallest needles, CO 54 (60, 64) sts, pm, and join rnd. Work 5 inches (approx 45 rows) in St st.

*Inc rnd: K1, M1, knit to end of rnd. Cont in St st, rep inc rnd every 5 (4, 3) rnds a total of 14 (20, 28)

times—68 (80, 92) sts. Cont even in St st until sleeve measures 20½ inches or to desired length, with a maximum circumference of 10 (11½, 13) inches. DO NOT BREAK YARN. Place last 20 (24, 30) sts just knit on st holder (these will later form underarm seams). Place rem sts either on spare needle or scrap yarn.

BODY

CO 75 (84, 90) st, pm, CO 75 (84, 90), pm. Join rnd.

Rnd 1: (K3, p3) to end of round.

Rnd 2: (P3, k3) to end of round.

Rep from * 7 times total (14 rows). This results in a 3 × 3 seed-stitch border along the bottom of the sweater.

Wrap Line Pattern

Rnd 15: K5, p3, knit to end of rnd.

Rnd 16: K5, k3, p3, knit to end of rnd.

Rnd 17: K6, p3, knit to end of rnd.

Rnd 18: K6, k3, p3, knit to end of rnd.

This pattern sequence repeats throughout the entire body. It will be assumed from this point that each knit round begins with a 6-st border, which shifts one st every other rnd (for example, on rnd 19, k7, p3, knit to end of rnd. On rnd 21, k8, etc.). This creates the diagonal line across the sweater, imitating a front wrap.

Continue working as established for 10 more rnds.

Rnd 29: K1, k2tog, knit to 3 sts before second marker, ssk, then knit rest of rnd.

Rnd 30: Knit rnd.

Rep from * 5 times total—140 (158, 170) sts.

K 22 (28, 32) rnds even.

Rnd 61 (66, 70): *K1, M1, knit to 1 st before second marker, M1, k1, knit rest of rnd.

Next rnd: K around.

Rep from * 5 times total (10 rows)—150 (168, 180) sts.

Cont in pat for 3 (8, 10) rnds. End established pat

and cont as written for each size as indicated:

For Size Small Only

Rnd 74: K34, p1, k3, p3, knit around.

Rnd 75: K36, p3, knit around.

Rnd 76: K33, p3, k3, p3, knit around.

Rnd 77: K35, p5, purl around.

Rnd 78: K32, p3, k2, M1, k3, p3, knit around.

For Size Medium Only

Rnd 84: K38, p2, k3, p3, knit around.

Rnd 85: K40, p4, knit around.

Rnd 86: K37, p3, k4, p3, knit around.

Rnd 87: K39, p6, knit around.

Rnd 88: K36, p3, k6, p3, knit around.

For Size Large Only

Rnd 90: K41, p2, k3, p3, knit around.

Rnd 91: K45, p4, knit around.

Rnd 92: K40, p3, k4, p3, knit around.

Rnd 93: K42, p6, knit around.

Rnd 94: K39, p3, k6, p3, knit around.

You have now established 2 opposing borders. Cut yarn, leaving long tail to work in later. Leaving markers as originally placed, shift needles so that points exit directly between 2 opposing wrap borders *(38 [42, 45] sts rem between marker and needle point on either size of your needle; 75 [84, 90] stitches across back of sweater, between markers)*. For the rest of sweater knit flat (not in the round), using a circular needle or set of dpns.

*Row 79 (89, 95) *(RS)*: P2tog, p2, knit across to last 4 sts, p2, p2tog.

Row 80 (90, 96) (WS): P3, k3, purl across to last 6 sts, k3, p3.

Row 81 (91, 97) (RS): P3, k3, knit across to last 3 sts, p3.

smaller circular needle or dpns. Work across left front of body in MC (including border pattern), until 1 st before the sleeve. *Pick up one sleeve and interchange last st of MC with first st of CC. Knit CC st with MC yarn, and then MC st with CC yarn.

Place both these sts on larger needle, then cont across sleeve with smaller needle and CC yarn. One st before end of sleeve, repeat process with next section of MC yarn, picking up new ball of MC yarn for back of the sweater. Rep from*, remembering to use separate balls of MC and CC yarn for each section (5 separate balls total).

Row 2 (WS): Cont in pat, working each "join" st in the opposing yarn, to ensure each row of yoke is securely connected. This applies to sections marked (k,p,k)CC as well, which require doubling back across sleeve sts.

Rep the following 8-row pat 6 (6, 7) times (beg with row 3 here, as rows 1 and 2 have been completed once):

Row 1 (RS): KMC and KCC across entire row.

Row 2 (WS): PMC and PCC across entire row.

Row 3: KMC, (k,p,k)CC, KMC, (k,p,k)CC, KMC.

Row 4: Rep row 2.

Row 5: Rep row 1.

Row 6: Rep row 2.

Row 7: KMC to last 2 sts, k2tog. Ssk first 2 sts of CC, KCC to last 2 sts, k2tog. Ssk first 2 sts of MC, KMC to last 2 sts, k2tog. Ssk first 2 sts of CC, KCC to last 2 sts, k2tog. Ssk first 2 sts of MC, KMC.

Row 8: Rep row 2.

For Sizes Medium and Large Only

On last row of above pat (row 8 of last rep), p2tog at beg and end of each sleeve, in CC.

Place entire body on smaller needles. Break CC yarns, leaving long tails to work in later. Break MC for back and right side of body. Leave left front body MC ball intact, cont around.

Row 82 (92, 98) (WS): P3, k3, purl across to last 6 sts, k3, p3.

Repeat 4-row pattern from * 9 times total (36 rows). Place 8 (10, 13) sts before each marker, and 7 (10, 12) sts after each marker on st holders. These sts will later form underarm seams.

YOKE

Join sleeves to body as follows:

Continue to work 6-st border on each side of V-neck as established above, dec every 4th row.

Starting with Row 1 (RS):

Place all live MC sts on larger circular needle or dpns, and place all live CC sts from sleeves on

RS rows: With MC, (k3, p3) across row.

WS rows: P3, k3) across row.

Work as established for 8 rows.

Row 9 (RS): *(K2tog, k1, p2tog, p1), repeat from * to end.

Row 10 (WS): BO loosely in pattern.

V-neck

Using smaller needle, RS facing, and CC, start just below collar and pick up 84 (84, 86) sts along left side of V-neck, 1 center st, and 84 (84, 86) sts along opposite side. Work 3 rows St st in CC yarn.

***Row 1 (WS):** Purl to 1 st before center st, p3tog, purl to end.

Row 2 (RS): Knit to 1 st before center st, k3tog, knit to end.

Repeat from * 8 times total (16 rows total).

Row 17: Rep row 1.

****Row 18 (RS):** Knit to 3 sts before center, k2tog, k3tog, k2tog, knit to end.

Row 19: P to 1 st before center st, p3tog, purl to end.

Rep from ** 8 (9, 10) times total.

Next row: Knit to 1 st before center st, k2tog, knit to end.

Divide sts in half along center line and seam together using CC and 3-needle bind off (see below).

FINISHING

Work in all loose ends. To finish underarms, use 3-needle bind off (see also page 22), noting special instructions for each size as indicated.

3-needle bind off: Turn sweater inside out. Place the MC and CC underarm sts on smaller needles. With the RS of the 2 pieces facing and the needles parallel, insert a third needle into the first st on each needle and knit them together. Knit the next 2 sts in the same way. Slip the first st on the third needle over the second st and off the needle.

Small: Every 3rd st, k2 CC sts into 1 MC st.

Medium: Every 4th st, k2 CC sts into 1 MC st.

Large: Every 5th st k2 CC sts into 1 MC st.

Rep until all underarm sts are bound off. Rep for other arm. Weave in loose ends.

Block sweater as necessary.

State champ,
3 years running.

Track Meet

athletic socks

KAREN H. BAUMER

There's something I love about the fact that these socks look just like the classic athletic socks you can buy at any run-of-the-mill department store—it's almost like a knitter's "in" joke. On the other hand, if you love the fit of hand-knit wool socks, why not make them from stretch cotton, too? Make the contrast stripes in your school's colors!

MATERIALS

Cascade Yarns Fixation (98.3% cotton, 1.7% elastic; 186 yds/50g [stretched]):

- 2 balls # 8001, White (MC)
- 1 ball #3628, Red (CC)

Set of five US size 6 (4mm) double-pointed needles

Tapestry needle

GAUGE

26 sts = 4 inches in St st

SIZES

Women's M (men's M)

FINISHED MEASUREMENTS

Cuff length to top of ankle: 8 inches

Foot length from back of heel to toe: 9 (10) inches

Foot and cuff circumference: 8 (8½) inches

Cool Tip

If sock cuffs or feet are lengthened beyond the men's size M, you may need additional yarn. Alternatively, work the toes in CC if you run short of MC.

CUFF

With MC and dpns, CO 52 (56) sts, divided evenly over 4 dpns—13 (14) sts per needle. Work k2,p2 rib for 1½ inches. Switch to CC and knit 1 rnd plain, then work 5 rnds in k2,p2 rib to line up with earlier rib. Switch to MC and knit 1 rnd plain, then work 4 rnds in established rib pattern. With CC, knit 1 rnd plain, 5 rnds in rib, cut CC leaving a tail to weave in later. With MC, knit 1 rnd plain and cont in established rib until cuff measures 8 inches from beg, ending after full rnd.

HEEL FLAP

Work heel flap over 26 (28) sts, leaving remaining sts on needles.

Row 1 (RS): *Sl1, k1, rep from * across, turn.

Row 2: Sl1, purl to end.

Rep rows 1 and 2 until flap measures 2½ (2¾) inches, ending with RS row.

Row 1 (WS): Sl1, p13 (14), p2tog, p1, turn.

Row 2 (RS): Sl1, k3, ssk, k1, turn.

Row 3: Sl1, p4, p2tog, p1, turn.

Row 4: Sl1, k5, ssk, k1, turn.

Row 5: Sl1, p6, p2tog, p1, turn.

Row 6: Sl1, k7, ssk, k1, turn.

Proceed in this fashion, inc by 1 the number of sts worked before the dec in each row, until all sts have been worked. Finish with a RS row—14 (16) sts rem on working needle.

GUSSET

Divide heel sts, leaving half on current needle and putting other half on empty needle. With RS of work facing, use needle holding leftmost heel sts to pick up sts along slipped stitched edge of heel flap, moving towards the cuff, picking up 17 (18) sts (needle 1).

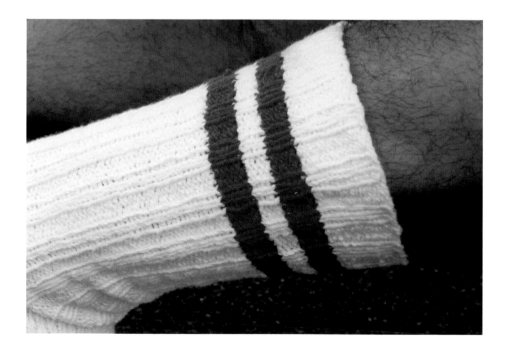

With empty needle, cont knitting across first needle of sts that have been "resting" during work on heel flap (needle 2). With new needle cont across rem needle with resting sts (needle 3). You are now at other side of heel flap. With empty needle (needle 4), proceed down heel flap by picking up 17 (18) sts, then cont across rem 7 (8) live sts on last needle—74 (80) sts total.

Gusset Shaping

Rnd 1: Knit around, knitting through back loop on the picked-up sts along both sides of the heel flap only; otherwise knit normally.

Rnd 2: Knit to last 3 sts on needle 1, k2 tog, k1; knit across needles 2 and 3; on needle 4, k1, ssk, knit to end.

Rnd 3: Knit.

Rep rnds 2 and 3 only until 52 (56) sts remain.

FOOT

Cont in St st until foot measures 7 (8) inches from back of heel (or until 2 inches short of desired length). Rejoin CC and work 1 row, cut CC. Continue with MC (or work remainder of toe in CC, if desired).

TOE DECREASES

Rnd 1: Needle 1—knit to last 3 sts, k2tog, k1; needle 2—k1, ssk, knit to end; needle 3—knit to last 3 sts, k2tog, k1; needle 4—k1, ssk, knit to end.

Rnd 2: Knit.

Rep these 2 rnds until 20 (24) sts remain, then proceed with rnd 1 only until 12 sts remain.

Knit across sts on needle 1. Place sts from needles 1 and 4 on one needle, st from needles 2 and 3 on second needle. Cut yarn, leaving about a 10- to 12-inch tail.

FINISHING

Graft toe: Hold two needles horizontally, one in front of the other, with top of sock facing you and tail of yarn attached to back needle (tail should hang from right end of needle from your current point of view).

1. With a tapestry needle, feed the tail purlwise through the rightmost st on the front needle. Pull yarn through and leave the st on the needle.

2. Insert needle knitwise through the rightmost st on the back needle. Pull yarn through and leave the st on the needle.

3. Insert needle knitwise through the rightmost st on the front needle and then slip that st off the needle. Insert needle purlwise through the next st on the front needle. Pull yarn through and leave st on needle.

4. Insert needle purlwise through rightmost st on back needle and then slip that st off the needle. Insert needle knitwise through the next st on back needle. Pull yarn through and leave st on needle.

Rep rows 3 and 4 only until all sts on both needles have been grafted together. The yarn should always stay below the needles as you work (i.e., not going over the tops of the needles and forming extra loops). Feed yarn through the last loop, then through to inside of sock.

Weave in remaining ends.

Je m'appelle
Veronique.
Et vous?

Exchange
Student

LEVEL: **J.V.**

eiffel tower dress

HANNAH HOWARD

Who doesn't love the French? The food, the art, the inexplicable and envied air of sophistication? This project was inspired by Francophiles and memories of semesters abroad.

MATERIALS

Berroco Softwist (41% wool, 59% rayon; 100 yds/50g):
- 10 balls #9420, Nouveau Berry (MC)
- 3 balls #9443, Smoothie (CC1)

Trendsetter Voila (100% nylon; 180 yds/50g):
- 1 ball #8284, light pink (CC2)

US size 6 (4.0mm) needles (or size needed to obtain gauge)

Size H crochet hook

Yarn needle

GAUGE

20 stitches and 24 rows = 4 inches in St st

SIZES

S/M (L/XL)

FINISHED MEASUREMENTS

Bust: 32 (33) inches

Hips: 34 (35) inches

Length: 30 inches

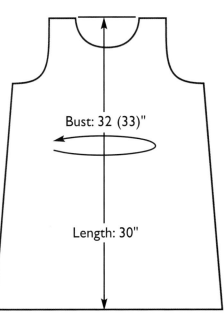

Bust: 32 (33)"

Length: 30"

Directions

FRONT

With MC, cast on 96 (100) sts. Work 3 rows in garter stitch (knit every row).

Rows 4–6: Beg with purl row, work in St st.

Rows 7–42: Add CC1, and cont in St st, work chart.

Skirt Shaping

Rows 43–44: BO 2 sts at beg of each row (92, 96 sts).

Row 45–58: Work chart.

Row 59: Dec 1 st at beg and end of row (90, 94 sts).

Row 60–74: Work chart.

Row 75: Dec 1 st at beg and end of row (88, 92 sts).

Rows 76–88: Work chart.

Row 89–90: BO 2 sts at beg and end of next 2 rows (84, 88 sts).

Row 91: Inc 1 st at beg and end of row (86, 90 sts).

Row 92–138: Work chart until piece measures 7½ inches from last increase.

Armhole Shaping

Rows 139–140: BO 6 sts at beg of each row (74, 78 sts).

Rows 141–144: Dec 1 st at beg and end of RS rows (70, 74 sts).

For Size Small only: *Rows 145–161:* Dec 1 st at beg and end of every RS row (52 sts).

For Size Large only: *Rows 145–161:* Dec 1 st at beg and end of every other RS row (64 sts).

Both sizes: Work 14 rows even.

Neck Shaping

K14 (16), BO 24 (32), knit rem 14 (16) sts. Place sts for one shoulder on st holder. Dec 1 st from neck edge every other row until 10 (12) sts remain. BO. Rep for second shoulder, reversing shaping.

BACK

With MC, CO 96 (100) sts. Work 3 rows in garter stitch.

Rows 4–14: Beg with purl row, work in St st.

Rows 15–180: Add CC1, work chart. Maintain all shaping as for front.

FINISHING

Weave in loose ends with tapestry needle. With right sides facing, seam together sides of garment using mattress stitch (see page 20). Sew shoulder seams. With crochet hook and CC2 double-stranded, sc edging (see page 21) around neck, armholes, and hem.

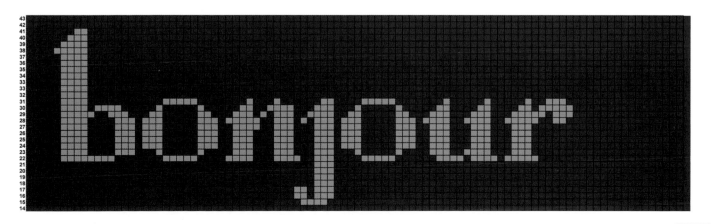

See you on the beach!

Spring Break

poolside bag

VICKIE HOWELL

Whether you're hitting the beach in Fort Lauderdale or are pool-bound in Vegas, a good tote bag is a spring break must-have. This version is knit from the same craft store plastic lacing that we used to make key chains at Girl Scout camp. It works up quickly, is waterproof, and best of all, the supplies to make it are so inexpensive that you'll be able to save your hard-earned cash to buy a matching bikini! Happy R&R!!

MATERIALS

Plastic craft lacing (100 yds/90m)
- 3 spools Blue/Green (MC)
- 1 spool Neon Green (CC)

US size 35 (19mm) circular needles, 29 inches in length

Tapestry needle

Clear plastic purse handles

GAUGE

8 sts = 4 inches

FINISHED MEASUREMENTS

12 x 16 inches

Directions

BASE

With MC, CO 3 sts. Knit 3 rows.

Next row: K1, M1, knit to end (4 sts).

Knit 3 rows.

Next row: K1, M1, knit to last st, M1, k1 (6 sts).

Knit 12 rows.

Next row: Ssk, k2, k2tog (4 sts).

Knit 3 rows.

Next row: K1, k2tog, k1 (3 sts).

Knit 2 rows. Do not cut lacing.

BODY

Keeping the 3 existing sts on needle, use MC to pick up 59 more sts around base (62 sts).

Knit all rnds even until piece measures 7 inches.

Join CC and knit until piece measures 10 inches.

Switch back to MC and knit 3 rnds.

Purl 2 rnds. BO purlwise.

FINISHING

Weave in ends. Plastic lacing is fairly slick, so you may need to knot some of the ends after weaving them in.

Fold over top edge where purling began and sew down, creating a hem approx 2 inches deep.

Using MC and tapestry needle, center handles and attach by wrapping lacing through handle holes and bag fabric several times.

Save our planet!
Recycle.

Granolas

save the skeins scarves

LISA SHOBHANA MASON

What do you do with hopelessly abandoned knitting projects and leftover yarn from completed projects? Recycle them into a Save the Skeins Scarf! Collect leftovers from your knitting pals. The more colors and textures, the better! If your stash is pretty basic, you might want to add skeins of something textured, something shiny, and something fuzzy. Since you don't need whole skeins, this is a great project to knit with a group of friends.

MATERIALS

Lots of leftover worsted or heavy worsted weight yarns (or two strands of thinner yarns held together)

Wide Version:

Cascade Yarns 220 Superwash (100% washable wool; 220 yds/100g): #851, Celery

Cascade Yarns Pearls, (55.7% cotton), 44.3% viscose; 130 yds/50g): #6388, Purple

Cascade Yarns Pima Tencel (50% Peruvian pima cotton/50% Tencel; 120 yds/50g): #7018, Teal

Berroco Crystal FX (100% nylon/146 yds/50g): #4704 Caribe

Berroco Medley (75% wool/15% acrylic/10% nylon; 73 yds/50g; #8913, Damarisotta Mix

Berroco Pleasure (66% angora/ 29% merino wool/5% nylon; 130 yds/50g): #8631, Rich Blue

Berroco Suede (100% nylon ribbon; 120 yds/50g): #3704, Wrangler

Stacy Charles Micio (60% polyamide, 40% wool; 110 yds/50g): #126, purple

Crystal Palace Yarns Fizz (100% polyester; 120 yds/50g): #9529, Scuba Dive

Crystal Palace Yarns Shag (45% wool/45% acrylic/10% Polyamide): #7198, Seven Seas

Mini Version:

Cascade Yarns Pearls (55.7% cotton, 44.3% viscose; 130 yds/50g): #6388, Purple

Berroco Crystal FX (100% nylon;146 yds/50g): #4708, Kir

Berroco Pleasure (66% angora/29% merino wool/ 5% nylon; 130 yds/50g): #8623, Primary Fuscia

Stacy Charles Micio, (60% polyamide/40% wool; 110 yds/50g): #125, pink

Tahki Yarns Shannon (100% wool; 92 yds/50g): #15, Purple

US size 9 (5.5mm) circular needle 24 or 29 inches in length (or size needed to obtain gauge)

FINISHED MEASUREMENTS

Wide Version: Approximately 6 (or desired width) x 72 inches

Mini Version: Approximately 3.5 (or desired width) x 60 inches

Directions

CO 200 (244) sts, leaving a 6-inch tail.

Use any combination of the stitch patterns. To change yarns, complete row, cut yarn, and leave a 6-inch tail. Tie an overhand knot using tail of yarn just cut and 6-inch tail of new yarn. Cont in this method until scarf width measures 3.5 (6) inches or desired width.

Stitch Patterns

SEED STITCH

Row 1 (RS): K1, *p1, k1; repeat from * to end.

Row 2 (WS): Knit the purl sts and purl the knit sts.

Rep row 2 for seed st.

GARTER STITCH

Row 1: Knit all stitches, every row.

OPENWORK STITCH

Row 1: K2 *(yo,sl1,k1,PSSO), rep from * to last 2 sts, k2.

Row 2: Knit all stitches.

DOUBLE MOSS

Rows 1 and 2: *K2, p2, rep from * to end of row.

Rows 3 and 4: *P2, k2*, rep from * to end of row.

Rep 4 rows for pat.

laptop & calculator sleeves

VICKIE HOWELL

Pockets aren't the only things that need protectors— our techie goods need them, too! Keep your laptop and calculator covered with one of these sleek little numbers. Duplicate stitch creates the mock-intarsia "Silicon" and "Pi" symbols that embellish each deceptively soft, metallic sleeve. These computer cozies put the "funk" in functional and knit up so fast you'll have a set done before your next trig test!

MATERIALS

Laptop Sleeve

Berroco Quest (100% nylon; 82 yds/50g):

- 3 balls #9825, Lapis (MC)
- 1 ball #9809, Silver (CC)

1-inch button

Calculator Sleeve

Berroco Quest (100% nylon; 82 yds/50g):

- 1 ball #9814, Tuxedo (MC)
- Small amount of #9825, Lapis (CC)

US size 8 (5mm) needles (or size needed to obtain gauge)

GAUGE

20 sts = 4 inches in St st

FINISHED MEASUREMENTS

Laptop Sleeve: 2 x 13¾ inches
Calculator Sleeve: 4 x 7 inches

"Silicon" Laptop Sleeve

With MC, CO 69 sts. Work 4 rows in garter st.

Next row: Beg working in St st, cont until piece measures 13¾ inches.

Next RS row: Work 5 sts in MC. Switch to CC, work 59 sts. Join second ball of MC and work last 5 sts. Cont in this manner, working the border in MC and the body in CC until piece measures 24¼ inches.

In MC ONLY, work 4 rows in garter st. BO.

FINISHING

Tab Closure

With MC, pick up 5 sts in center of top back edge (32 sts in from either side). Work in garter st until tab measures 2½ inches.

Next RS row (buttonhole row): K2, yo, k2tog, k1.

Cont in garter st for 4 more rows. BO.

Using MC and tapestry needle, duplicate stitch "Si," and backstitch numbers onto "front" half of sleeve.

Fold in half and sew side seams. Sew on button.

"Pi" Calculator Sleeve

With MC, CO 20 sts. Work 4 rows in garter st.

Next row: Begin working in St st, cont until piece measures 14½ inches.

Work last 4 rows in garter st. BO.

Using CC and tapestry needle, duplicate stitch the "Pi" symbol and backstitch the numbers onto "front" half of sleeve.

Fold in half and sew side seams.

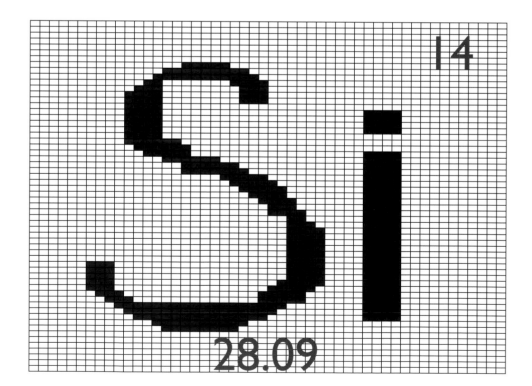

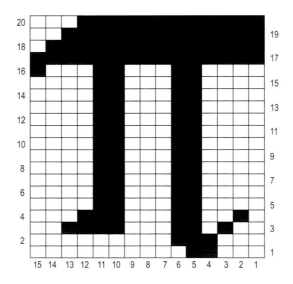

Senior Brass kicks A--!

Marching Band

LEVEL: **J.V.**

fingerless gloves

LORI STEINBERG

I thought about the chilly hands of my teenage marching band friends past and present during those crisp, fall football games, parades, and pep rallies. Wouldn't it be nice to keep warm and still be able to play, or even to make a call on your cell phone? I chose Crystal Palace Merino Frappe yarn because the bulky look is hip and gender neutral and its lightness leaves your fingers flexible. Make a school-colors pair to match your uniform, and you'll be the envy of the entire brass section!

MATERIALS

Crystal Palace Yarns Merino
   Frappe (80% merino wool/
   20% nylon; 140 yds/50g):

- 1 skein #122, Deep
   Variegated Purple

US size 5 (3.75mm) set of 4
   double-pointed needles (or
   size needed to obtain gauge)

Tapestry needle

Scrap yarn to hold stitches

SIZES

M (L)

GAUGE

20 sts = 4 inches in Broken Rib
   pattern

Directions

Broken Rib Pattern (BR)

Rnds 1 and 2: Knit.

Rnds 3 and 4: K2, p2. Twist yarns on WS to prevent holes in work.

Left-Hand Glove

CO 36 sts, spread evenly across 3 dpns. Join rnd. K2, p2 for 3 (3½) inches. Beg BR pat, work 1 rnd to last 4 sts, pm, k2, p1, k1. Rep last rnd, slipping marker on every rnd.

Next rnd: K2, p2 to marker.

Begin incs for thumb gusset: K1, m1, k1, p1, m1, k1.

Cool Tip

You have plenty of yarn, even if you're knitting the larger size, so leave generous tails with bind-offs and cast-ons for weaving in later.

Next rnd: K2, p2 to marker, then k3, p2, k1. Cont in BR pat. Knit thumb gusset in k2, p2 rib, maintaining 1 knit stitch at each end, incr in pattern every 4th row until there are 8 sts between the 2 end sts.

Work 1 more rnd in pat to marker. Drop marker and k1, slip next 8 sts onto spare scrap of yarn, CO 2 sts, purl last st from rnd. Cont in BR pat until 1½ (1¾) inches above CO over thumb opening, or until glove hits bottoms of fingers where they separate.

FIRST FINGER

K2, p2, k1, CO 2 (3), slip next 26 sts to piece of scrap yarn, p1, k2, p2. Distribute 12 (13) sts evenly on 3 needles.

Next rnd: k2, p2, k2, p2 (3), k2, p2. Cont as established until finger measures 1 (1¼) inches or to knuckle. BO in pat.

SECOND FINGER

Slip first 4 sts from scrap yarn to empty needle, slip last 4 sts from scrap yarn to another empty needle. With third needle, rejoin yarn and pick up and knit 2 (3) sts over CO sts of first finger. K1, p2, k1 from first spare needle, CO 2 sts, p1, k2, p1 from second spare needle.

Next rnd: p1 (2), (k2, p2) twice, k2, p1. Distribute the 12 (13) sts comfortably on 3 needles. Cont as established until finger measures 1¼ (1½) inches or to knuckle. BO in pat.

THIRD FINGER

Work same as second finger, BO off after 1 (1¼) inches.

LITTLE FINGER

Slip rem 10 sts to 2 needles. Rejoining yarn, pick up 2 sts over CO for third finger. K1, p2, K2, p2, K2, p1.

Next rnd: p1, (k2, p2) twice, k2, p1. Distribute sts comfortably on 3 needles. Cont as established until finger measures 1 (1¼) inches or desired length to knuckle. BO in pat.

THUMB

Slip 8 gusset sts to 2 needles. Rejoining yarn, pick up and knit 5 sts over CO sts.

Next rnd: (p2,k2) twice, p3, k2. Cont as established for 1 (1¼) inches.BO in pat.

Right-Hand Glove

Work same as for left-hand glove to first finger, ending last rnd 4 sts before end of rnd—these 4 sts are first sts of finger.

FIRST FINGER

K2, p2, k1, cast on 2(3) sts, slip next 26 sts to scrap yarn, on new needle k2, p2, k1.

Next rnd: k1, p2 (3), k2, p2, k2, p2, k1. Cont as established for 1 (1¼) inches.
BO in pat.

SECOND FINGER

Slip 4 sts from each end of scrap to 2 empty needles. Rejoin yarn and with a third needle pick up and k2 (3) sts over CO sts of first finger. K1, p2, k2, CO 2 sts, p1, k2, p1.

Next rnd: P1 (2), (k2, p2) twice, k2, p1.

Cont as established until

finger measures 1 (1¼) inches.
BO in pat.

Complete rem fingers according to directions for left-hand glove.

FINISHING

Turn inside out to weave in all ends. (If you try to weave in ends from right side, you will stretch finger tops unnecessarily.) Use tails to close holes at joins of fingers and to even out BO edges. Press lightly on wrong side under damp cloth.

Band practice tonight.
Rachel's garage.
Be there!

Rockers

chevron guitar strap

VICKIE HOWELL

When I was in my late teens I dreamed of starting a band called "Why Barbie's Bad." I bought a bass (which I later sold to pay rent) and then a guitar, which I still have to this day. (In fact, the model borrowed it for this picture.) Although I never actually learned how to play more than a couple of riffs and my band never got past the planning stage, I still consider myself a closet rock star. Since my knitting abilities far exceed my musical prowess, I've designed a few guitar straps over the years as a tribute to my favorite musicians. This version uses chevrons to create a funky strap that's neither too masculine nor too feminine. Knit a few of these in different colors to suit your changing moods, and remember, any guitar worth playing is a guitar worth accessorizing!

MATERIALS

Lion Brand Glitterspun (60% acrylic/ 27% Cupro/13% polyester; 115 yds/105m per 50g):
- 1 ball #153, Onyx (MC)
- 1 ball #150, Silver (CC1)

Lion Brand Fun Fur (100% polyester; 57 yds/52m per 40g):
- 1 ball Black (CC2)

US size 6(4.0mm) needles (or size needed to obtain gauge)

Size G crochet hook

Tapestry needle

Leather or vinyl strap tabs (recycled from old guitar strap)

Black thread

Sewing needle

GAUGE

20sts x 24 rows = 4 inches in St st

FINISHED MEASUREMENTS

2½ inches wide × desired length

Directions

> **Chevron Pattern Stitch**
> **(12 rows)**
>
> *Row 1:* K1, inc1, k5, ssk, k2tog, k5, inc1, k1.
>
> *Row 2:* Purl.
>
> Rep these 2 rows 5 more times.

Cool Tip

Before you begin, determine how long you want your guitar strap to be. Measure an existing strap or ask a friend to help you by measuring from peg to neck while you hold your guitar in the position that's comfortable.

With MC, CO 8 sts. Work even in St st for 2 inches.

Next row (RS): Inc (by knitting into the st below) 4 sts evenly across row (12 sts).

Next row (WS): Purl.

Next row: Inc (by knitting into the st below) 4 sts evenly across row (16 sts).

Next row: Purl.

Cont with MC, begin working 12-row Chevron Stitch pat.

Next RS row: Switch to CC, repeat 12-row pattern.

Cont in this manner, alternating MC and CC1, until strap is 2½ inches shorter than desired length.

Next RS row: Dec (using k2tog) 4 sts evenly across row (12 sts).

Next row: Purl.

RS: Dec (using k2tog) 4 sts evenly across row (8 sts).

Work even in St st for 2 inches.

FINISHING

Weave in ends. Using CC2 and crochet hook, sc (see page 21) border down both sides of strap (not including tab area).

Attach strap tabs either by sewing them on with needle and thread or by drawing knitted end through plastic piece attached to leather/vinyl tab and sewing down with tapestry needle and CC.

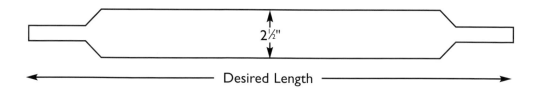

2½"

Desired Length

Starry Nights,
sparkly shawl.

Prom

LEVEL: **J.V.**

glittery wrap

KAREN H. BAUMER

This wrap uses a simple ladder lace pattern for maximum elegance with minimal effort. For a custom look, you could make the fringe with silk or satin ribbon to match your dress. The lace stretches a lot widthwise, so don't worry if your piece feels too skinny as you work. Blocking will widen it and maximize the lace effect.

MATERIALS

Berroco Metallic FX (85% rayon/15% metallic; 85yds/25g):
 • 8 hanks #1002, Silver

US size 8 (5.0mm) needles

Tapestry needle

Crochet hook for adding fringe (optional)

GAUGE

14 sts = 4 inches in pat st, blocked

FINISHED MEASUREMENTS

22 × 48 inches (64 inches including fringe)

Directions

CO 78 sts. Purl 1 row (WS).

Row 2 (RS): K1, *(SKPO, 2yo, k2tog), rep from * to last st, k1.

Row 3 (WS): *(P3, k1), rep from * to last 2 sts, p2.

Rep rows 2 and 3 until you have used up almost 7 hanks of yarn, then BO loosely on RS. Piece should measure approximately 12 × 26 inches when relaxed.

FINISHING

Weave in ends securely using tapestry needle. Block piece to finished measurements.

Cut 16-inch lengths for tassel fringe from last remaining hank of yarn and attach (see page 18), two at a time, to short edges of wrap to make 8-inch fringe. (If longer fringe is desired, purchase an additional hank of yarn.)

It's like a yearbook for your wrist!

Yearbook Staff

wire photo bracelet

JENNIFER PERKINS & VICKIE HOWELL

Keeping your friends close at all times is the only way to go, but who wants to carry around one of those bulky photo wallets? Not us; no way. Clearly, the better alternative is to accessorize, so we decided to combine our knitting and jewelry-making skills to create a cool wire cuff that's the perfect backdrop for your best pals' portraits!

MATERIALS

1 spool .28 gauge jewelry wire

US size 5 (3.75mm) needles

Tapestry needle

Shrink plastic paper

Yearbook

Computer

Scanner

Pinking shears

Drill with small bit

Small jump rings

Oven

Clear spray paint

Lobster clasp

Pliers

GAUGE

16 sts = 4 inches in garter stitch

SIZE

Fits up to a 7-inch wrist

FINISHED MEASUREMENTS

2½ × 6 inches (not including clasp)

Bracelet

Using needles and wire, CO 10 sts. Work even in garter stitch (knit all rows) until piece measures 6 inches OR about an inch shorter than your wrist measurement. BO.

Charms

Choose 6 of your very best friends. Find their photos in your yearbook. Scan the photos into your computer and, using any standard photo-editing software, crop the pictures to double the desired, finished size. Print out on shrink plastic paper, following manufacturer's instructions closely. To lighten photo, for example, print on transparency setting.

Once your pictures are printed, cut them out with pinking shears. Normal scissors are fine and dandy, but pinking shears will give the squares a fun edge and frame. Following shrink plastic instructions, cook charms in oven. When done and cooled, drill small holes in top of each charm with a drill. Take charms to a well-ventilated area and coat twice with clear spray paint, allowing them to dry completely between coats.

FINISHING

Using a tapestry needle, weave in ends. You may need to wrap wire into place to secure. Snip off excess with scissors or wire cutters.

When second coat of spray paint is completely dry, lay out charms on your bracelet and select a pattern that tickles your fancy. Using small jump rings and pliers, attach picture charms to bracelet by running jump rings through charms and into the holes in he bracelet.

The finishing touch will be adding a clasp to the bracelet. On one end, add two jump rings and a lobster clasp. In the center of the other side, add three jump rings interlocked.

Yearbook Staff

Knitty Wentworth
Buys wool but prefers cashmere.

Hope to KIP with you soon!

Guy Stitchie
*Voted: Best Looking
(in a ribbed pull-over)*

*Have a great summer!
K/E/F*

Clark Cable
Knit University scholarship winner.

Raven Knitshade
Enjoys playing with pointy sticks.

Lacey Purl
*Voted: Most Flirtatious
(likes knitting ruffles)*

Don't forget to write.

Send pictures of your WIPs!

Greg Needler
Valeknitorian

Can you believe we made it through the whole year without any UFOs? We rock!

Steven "Slip Stitch" Cunningham
Awarded Nobel Piece Prize for best knitted project.

Cass Onnanoff
Not afraid to drop stitches.

See you at Knit Nite!

We're outta here!

Graduation

class tassel hat

JACLYN CUNNINGHAM

Born and bred in the Northeast, I've always loved the multicolored and brightly patterned ski hats that dot the slopes each winter. With intarsia and Fair Isle styles back in fashion, I couldn't resist adapting those looks to create a ski hat that shows pride in your school colors and graduating class.

MATERIALS

Cascade Yarns 220 (100% Peruvian Wool; 220 yds/100g):
- 2 skeins #9457, Royal Blue (MC)
- 2 skeins #7827, Bright Yellow (CC)

US size 6 (4.0mm) circular 16-inch needle (or size needed to obtain gauge)

US size 8 (5.0mm) circular 16-inch needle (or size needed to obtain gauge)

US size 8 (5.0mm) set of 5 double-pointed needles (or size needed to obtain gauge)

Tapestry needle

GAUGE

4¼ sts = 4 inches in St st, using larger circular needle

SIZE

One size fits all

FINISHED MEASUREMENTS

18- to 20-inch circumference (depending on blocking)

10 inches deep, without cord and tassle

With MC and smaller circ nl, CO 88 sts and join rnd. Work 6 rnds in k2,p2 rib.

Rnd 7: Switch to larger circular needle. *K8, M1, rep from * to end of rnd (99 sts).

Rnd 8: Knit all sts.

Rnd 9: With CC, k all sts.

Rnds 10–20: Beg chart for color work pattern, reading from right to left, k all sts in each chart row (11 rows total for chart).

Rnds 21–22: With CC, knit size size size all sts.

Rnd 23: *K3 with MC, k1 with CC, rep from * to end of row.

Rnd 24–26: With MC, knit all sts (3 rnds).

Rnd 27: *K1 with MC, k1 with CC, k2 with MC, rep from * to end of row.

Rnd 28–30: With MC, knit all sts (3 rnds).

Rep rnds 23–30 until hat measures approximately 7 inches.

Begin Decreasing

Cont to work in color pat while dec.

Knit 1 rnd, placing a st marker after every 25th st, so hat sections are divided as evenly as possible.

> **Note:** there will be only 24 stitches in the last section.

On each row, knit all sts until 2 sts before each st marker, k2tog.

Cont dec until only 4 sts rem, 1 on each needle, switching to dpns when piece becomes too small for circular needle. Do not break CC after last color rnd before final dec. Leave tail connected to the yarn ball, draw out through top of hat.

Cord
(I-Cord Method)

Transfer 4 rem sts to dpn. Using CC still connected to piece, knit I-cord (as described on page 17) for approx 5 inches or to desired length. To end I-cord, break yarn and thread through all 4 sts on needle, and run through center of I-cord.

Alternate Cord
(For Thinner Cord)

BO top of hat by running MC through 4 rem sts. Leaving 15 inches of tail, break CC running through top of hat. Cut 2 additional 15-inch lengths of CC yarn, and tie to original strand of CC on inside of hat. After these two pieces are secured, draw through hole in top of hat. Braid three strands of yarn together until desired length. Attach to tassel as described below.

Tassel

Make tassel (see page 19) and attach to cord, sewing with tapestry needle and waste CC, tucking in ends.

FINISHING

Weave in all loose ends. Block to desired fit.

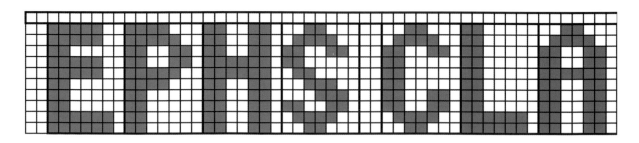

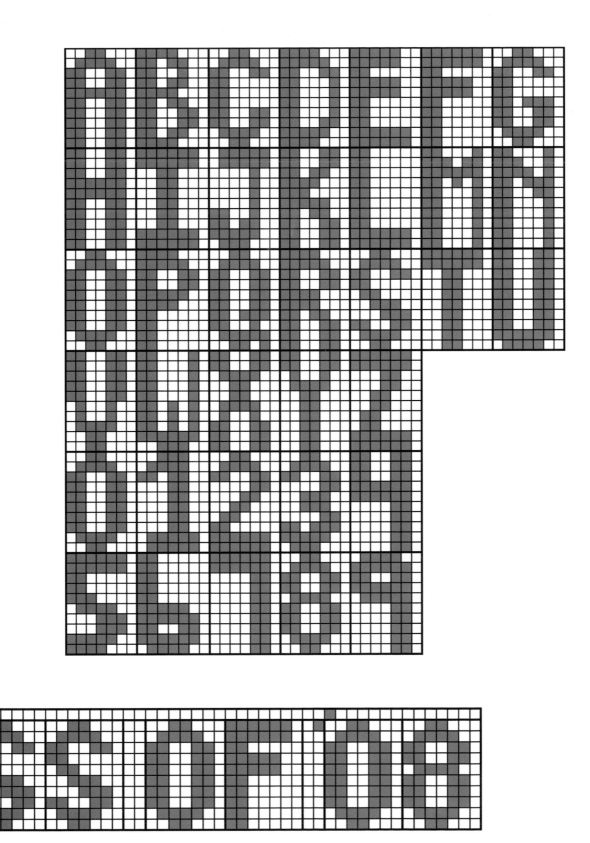

My dorm is going
to be sweeeet!

College Bound

dorm decor pillow & lampshade

VICKIE HOWELL

College dorms are pretty standard issue in their style, but the way that they're decorated doesn't have to be. Make your side of the room feel like home with this super-funky lampshade and pillow set.

MATERIALS

PILLOW

Crystal Palace Yarns Deco-Ribbon (30% nylon/70% acrylic; 80 yds/50g):

- 2 balls color #109 (MC)

Crystal Palace Yarns Shag (45% wool/45% acrylic/ 10% Polyamide):

- 2 balls Ebony (CC)

16-inch square pillow form

LAMPSHADE

Crystal Palace Yarns Deco-Ribbon (30% nylon/70% acrylic; 80 yds/50g):

- 2 balls color #109 (MC)

Crystal Palace Yarns Shag (45% wool/45% acrylic/10% polyamide):

- 1 ball Ebony (CC)

10-inch square lampshade top & bottom wires

Approx 8 binder clips or clothespins

BOTH

US size 10½ (6.5mm) needles (or size needed to obtain gauge)

Large-eyed tapestry needle

GAUGE

12 sts = 4 inches in MC and St st

FINISHED MEASUREMENTS

Pillow: 16 x 16 inches

Lampshade: 14 inches high

Pillow

With MC, CO 48 sts. Work 4 inches even in St st.

Next RS row: Join in CC and work 2 rows.

Switch back to MC, knit 1 row.

Next row (WS): *P1, yo 3 times, rep from * to end.

Next row: Knit the purled sts, drop the yos.

Work even in St st for 4 more inches.

Switch to CC and work 2 rows.

With MC, cont in St st for 4 inches.

With CC, work even in St st for 4 inches.

With MC, work 4 rows in St st.

With CC, work even in St st for 7 inches.

Work 4 rows in MC.

Work 4 more inches in CC. BO.

FINISHING

Fold piece in half widthwise and sew side seams using mattress stitch (see page 20), leaving top end open. Insert pillow form and sew opening.

Lampshade

With MC, CO 96 sts. Work even in St st for 3 inches.

Join CC, and work 4 rows in St st. Cut CC.

Next row (RS): Switch back to MC and knit 1 row.

Next row (WS): *P1, yo 3 times, repeat from * to end.

Next row: Knit the purled sts, drop the yos.

Work even in St st for 2 inches more.

Next RS row: Rejoin CC and work 4 rows in St st.

Next row (RS): Switch to MC and knit 1 row.

Next row (WS): *P1, yo 3 times, repeat from * to end.

Next row: Knit the purled sts, drop the yos.

Work even in St st for 3 more inches. BO.

FINISHING

With right sides facing, sew back seam to create tube.

Using clothespins or binder clips, attach shade in place around top shade wire. Using MC and tapestry needle, sew on shade by wrapping yarn around top wire all the way around square. Rep with bottom square wire. Place shade on lamp halo and secure with washer or finial.

Knitting Club

The best things in life are usually made better when shared with friends, and knitting is no exception. Community is one of the many cool things that knitting has to offer, and crafty groups are a great way to swap tips, show off projects, find inspiration, and meet new people. If you make a mistake on a project, someone from your "Knit Club" can likely help you fix it. If you want to model your new felted bag, your fellow knitsters will gladly be your audience. Whether you're an experienced stitcher, or someone who's new to the needles, you're bound to enjoy hanging out with others who know their knit. Here are five tips on how to start your own club:

1. Start an online "knitlist." The Internet is a group leader's best friend. These lists are the most efficient method for posting meeting information, knit-related questions, and pictures of finished objects (aka FOs). I recommend making it a "members only" group that requires moderator approval to join. This will help prevent spam and other unwanted, off-topic postings.

2. Find a meeting venue. Places like libraries, coffee shops, bookstores (as long as they have a café), or community centers all make great meeting places for a group like this. Make sure you choose a location with comfortable seating, plenty of light, and space to accommodate at least ten people. Check with the store manager or other powers that be to make sure that they're open to having your group meet there on a regular basis.

3. Pick a meeting day and time and stick to it. You'll find that your group is much more likely to flourish if people know they can count on meetings being held at the same time, on the same day, and in the same place. People often think for a while about attending before they actually do. It helps if they know you'll be there when they finally do decide to come.

4. Spread the word. Make fliers for your group and post them around schools, at local stores, on community boards, and the like. Try asking your local craft or yarn store owner whether you can leave a stack of them on the sales counter for interested patrons to grab.

5. Keep it fresh. In addition to your regularly scheduled meetings, plan a few off-site activities for your group. Combining knitting with holiday parties (including a handmade gift swap), BBQs in the park, train rides, and sleepovers are all great ways to perpetuate excitement about the club. Have fun!!

Faculty (our contributors)

Jenna Adorno

Preppies • Polo Shirt (Page 26)

Jenna is a knitter of all things, although her true passion is designing patterns for hip, stylish garments that really fit. She lives in Seattle and works in the software industry by day, but dreams of being paid fabulously to design knit garments full-time.

Chris Bahls

Jocks • Varsity Jacket (Page 46)

Chris is just a guy from a trailer park with a dream. He lives in Fullerton, California, works as a programmer, knits when he can, and visits the rodeo often.

Karen Baumer

Prom • Glittery Wrap (Page 108)

Track Meet • Athletic Socks (Page 82)

Karen is a linguist who lives in the San Francisco area and loves knitting, sewing, cooking, running, horses, Mozart's operas, and Bob Dylan. For some reason, Vickie likes to call her "Fancy Pants."

Jaclyn Cunningham

Graduation • Class Tassel Hat (Page 114)

Jaclyn picked up knitting in the summer of 2004, as a way to keep her hands busy while listening to Red Sox games on the radio each night and quickly became obsessed with the craft. She lives and knits in South Boston, Massachusetts, where she also works in publishing as a financial analyst.

Hannah Howard

Foreign Exchange Student • Eiffel Tower Dress (Page 86)

Hannah Howard is a designer/writer/fairy princess/astronaut. She's a cofounder of the crafting collective, Department of Craft (www.departmentofcraft.com) and an active member of the New York chapter of the Church of Craft.

Stefanie Japel

Homecoming Queen • Award Sash (Page 58)

Stefanie Japel is a scientist who lives out her rock 'n' roll dreams by designing funky knitwear. Visit her Web site (www.Glampyre.com) for more info.

Lisa Shobhana Mason

Granolas • Save the Skeins Scarves (Page 92)

Lisa is an intuitive counselor and astrologer who has made a secondary profession out of her primary obsession, knitting. She lives in Austin, Texas, teaches knitting classes, and creates one-of-a-kind and limited run pieces of knitwear. She sells her wares at www.scarletchickadee.com.

Betsy McCall

First Car • Car Cozies (Page 34)

Betsy designs for Crystal Palace Yarns, owns ShizKnits.com, and can be found toodling around the San Francisco Bay area in "Tang," her finely accessorized orange Karmann Ghia. When she's not knitting or designing, she spins round and round as a synchronized swimmer and poi firedancer.

Jillian Moreno for the Acme Knitting Company

Skaters • Crewneck Pullover (Page 38)

Jillian has never been on a skateboard, but tries to knit without limits. She lives in Ann Arbor, Michigan.

Melinda Morrow

Goths • Bat Shawl (Page 54)

Melinda started knitting four years ago. She lives in Seattle and teaches college English classes to fund her knitting and spinning projects.

Stephanie Mrse

Pep Rally • School Colors Scarf & Mittens (Page 50)

Stephanie lives in San Diego, California with her husband, Anthony, and her new baby, Henry. When she's not knitting, she's sewing, cross stitching, reading, or cooking.

Jenifer Paulousky

Dance Company • Wrap Sweater & Leg Warmers (Page 76)

Jenifer is an engineer and owner of Blue Alvarez Designs. She lives near Boston, Massachusetts with her partner, guitar, and enormous piles of yarn. Her line of knitwear and clothing can be found at www.bluealvarez.com.

Jennifer Perkins

Yearbook Staff • Photo Wire Bracelet (Page 109)

Jennifer Perkins is the woman behind the jewelry Web site Naughty Secretary Club. The Texas native is a founding member of the Austin Craft Mafia, host of Craft Lab and one of the hosts of DIY Network's *Stylelicious*.

William Shakespeare

Macbeth, Hamlet, Two Gentlemen of Verona, etc.

William was a busy and successful 16th century playwright. In his spare time, when not overseeing productions at London's Globe Theatre, he enjoyed writing sonnets.

Lori Steinberg

Drama Club • Theater Mask Hats (Page 70)

Marching Band • Fingerless Gloves (Page 100)

Lori directs plays and musicals in New York City. She was a stage bum as a teenager and hung out with a group of artistic young men and women whom she hopes to honor with her designs in this book.

Acknowledgments

This book was written during a particularly tumultuous time in my life. Its completion wouldn't have been possible without the support, encouragement, and hard work of many incredible people. My first choice for expressing appreciation to these kind folks would be through interpretive dance, but unfortunately, that wouldn't translate well onto paper. My second choice, of course, is haiku:

Oh, friends and colleagues
you are my knitspiration
Without you, I cry.

Since that seems a wee bit too dramatic for a knitting book (even for one of mine), I think I'll just communicate my gratitude the old-school way:

Thank you so much to the amazing team at Sterling Publishing for making my experience such a positive one and for giving me the opportunity to do something that I love. I especially want to thank: **Jo Fagan**, for your willingness to pitch all of my wacky ideas to the powers that be—I've really enjoyed getting to know you over the past couple of years and look forward to continuing to work together; **Rodman Neumann** for your patience and attention to detail; **Kelly Galvin** and **Chris Vacarri** for holding my publicity hand.

I am truly indebted to the companies who supplied the yarn for this book, and to my agent,

Sarah Sockit, for your guidance on a project that you weren't technically even getting paid for. Your insight means a great deal to me.

The novelty of this book's theme would never have worked if it weren't for the contributing designers' willingness to humor my vision. I'm honored and proud to have worked with you all. You are truly creative, magnificent people.

Jody Horton (aka J-Man, J-Dawg, Jackamo, or Jodediah), your mad photography skillz paired with your wicked **Steve Perry** and **Neil Diamond** impersonations, made our schedule-intense photo shoots completely entertaining. You're an absolute pleasure to work with—Don't Stop Believin'! **Abby Jones**, the most delightful photo assistant

ever, thanks for filling the positions of everything from gofer to model. You're a doll! **Karly Hand**, my dear friend and Photography coordinator extraordinaire, against budgetary and timeline odds, you did a spectacular job of making the shoots happen. To say that you worked your butt off would be an understatement. I really appreciate it!

To the models: **Rachelle Smith, Nicolas Cortez, Laura Lynde, Amy Scroggins, Chantal Barlow, Bobbie Ragsdale, Wes Meyers, Alex Wilson, Niki Nash, Kelsey Buaas** (and your mom, **Barbie!**), **Charmecia Burrell, Larry Hines, Star Silva, Lucas Anderson**, and **Nick Lebo**—thank you so much for donating your time and faces to this project. You were all so patient with our demands and in some cases totally saved us by filling in on a moment's notice. You guys rock!

I'd also like to give a shout out to **Baker School**, **Bowie High School** (especially **Principal Kent**, **Howard Cary**, and **Ms. Scott**) and **Alan Pogue** for letting us use your establishments for photography. It was so kind of you to let our team invade your space. Special thanks to **Parts & Labour**, **All Dressed Up and Shy**, and **Naughty Secretary Club** for letting us ambush you and borrow your wares for the "Popular" shoot, and to **Joel Rizor**, **Alessandra Ascoli**, and the rest of the **Screen Door Entertainment** and *Knitty Gritty* crew for your continued encouragement of all my endeavors.

On a more personal note, thank you so much to my inner sanctum of friends and family. Did you ever know that you're my heroes? Seriously, though, I owe you all so much, especially my mom (**Libby Bailey**) and my brother (**Kevin Montoya**) for being my constants, my rocks. To **Clint Howell** for going above and beyond the call of duty by helping me to get this book done—you're a lifesaver!, my dad (**Chuck Montoya**) for being there for me

when I least expected it, **Sacha Bryant** for twenty-two years of friendship and the memories of our infamous high school years of which I couldn't help thinking during this project, and, along with **Bret McCarroll** and **Jenny Provin**, thanks for allowing me to make your yearbook pictures public. It takes a special kind of person to be okay with that.

To my B/F/Fs, **Tammy Izbicki**, for your unconditional love and absolute friendship, and **Kevin Iudicello** (who will hate that I worked the term "B/F/F" and his name into the same sentence), for your priceless sarcasm and genuine interest in understanding how a person can make a living out of crafting. To my nonbiological twin, **Steve Bae**, for your brilliant brainstorming via instant messenger; **Darren Metzger** for your thoughtfulness both personally and professionally; my *Stylelicious* girls (aka **Austin Craft Mafia**) for being a constant source of inspiration to me; **Jenny Medford** for letting me camp out at your house with my laptop while our kids played together; to **Lori Steinberg** for letting me stay with you while I was meeting with the publishers in New York and for taking some of the knitting burden off my

shoulders; and to **Karen Baumer** for being on the receiving end of the knitting question "Bat Phone"—your advice is invaluable to me. Along with **Karen** and **Lori**, I'd also like to mention the rest of the MEOWers: **Stephanie**, **Tiffany**, **Chris**, **Deb**, **Debbie**, **Kristen**, **Claudia**, **Melinda**, **Sarah**, **Jenn**, **Susan**, and **Martha**. Our little knitlist life and crafty commentary postings have become a staple in my life and you have all become like family. Thank you for all that you do.

Finally, to **Tanner** and **Tristan** for doing such a good job of playing at home and letting me work, while you likely would've much preferred to be at the park. I know that having a mommy who often does her job from home is both a blessing and a curse. I'm so thankful to have two such extraordinary little sidekicks to keep me company. It's hard for me to believe that you'll both be teenagers yourselves someday, but I look forward to being with you every step of the way. I'm so proud of you.

This book was actualized while watching **John Hughes** movies and listening to the sound tracks from *Pretty in Pink*, *Garden State*, and *Napoleon Dynamite*.

About the Photographer

Jody strikes a pose during 'Dance Company' shoot

Jody Horton is a photographer and filmmaker. He is founder and director of Corduroy Pictures, a design, video, and photo studio based in Austin, Texas. To see more of his work, please visit www.corduroypictures.com.

About the Author

Vickie primps model's hair for "Punk" shoot.

A self-proclaimed crafty gRRRL, **Vickie Howell** has been involved in the creative arts for as long as she can remember. Before becoming the mother of two boys, she worked in the entertainment industry at companies including International Creative Management (ICM) and Alliance Atlantis Entertainment. Post-motherhood, she has founded three crafty Web-based businesses and two Stitch 'n' Bitch groups. She is the host of television's *Knitty Gritty*, co-host of DIY Network's *Stylelicious*, and a founding member of the infamous Austin Craft Mafia. She writes a regular column for *Vogue Knit.1* magazine. More of her designs can be found in her first book, *New Knits on the Block*, as well as a variety of publications nationwide. Vickie lives, breathes, and knits in Austin, Texas. For more info, check out www.vickiehowell.com.

Index